FORGET WALL STREET!

FORGET WALL STREET!

Go For the
Gold
(and Silver Too)

KERRY H. LUTZ

ISBN: 978-0615642352

Dedication

This book is dedicated to my father, Nat Lutz. His wisdom, his knack for aphorisms and his ceaseless good humor, dry wit and patience have helped me to become almost half the man he was. And in this situation, half really is good enough.

Acknowledgements

In a book such as this one, there are always too many people who've contributed to properly acknowledge them all. Here's an abbreviated list of contributors to my daily radio show on www.FinancialSurvivalNetwork. com.

Tyler Gallagher	www.regalassets.com
Bob Chapman (RIP)	www.internationalforcecaster.com
Doug Casey	www.caseyresearch.com
Ed Steer	www.caseyresearch.com/gsd
David Morgan	www.silver-investor.com
Jim Sinclair	www.jsmineset.com
Mickey Fulp	www.mercinarygeologist.com
Ron Hera	www.heraresearch.com
Jay Taylor	www.jaytaylormedia.com
Chris Waltzek	http://radio.goldseek.com
Rick Ackerman	www.rickackerman.com
Chris Duane	www.dont-tread-on.me
Gary Gibson	www.dollarvigilante.com
Jeff Berwick	www.dollarvigilante.com
Darryl R. Schoon	www.drschoon.com
Greg McCoach	www.gregmccoach.com
John Rubino	www.dollarcollapse.com
Mike Mish Shedlock	http://globaleconomicanalysis.blogspot.com/
Diana Zoppa	www.zoppamedia.com
"Ranting" Andy Hoffman	www.milesfranklin.com
Danielle Park	www.jugglingdynamite.com
Peter Grandich	www.grandich.com
Bix Weir	www.roadtoroota.com
Bill Murphy	www.gata.org
Gerald Celente	www.trendsjournal.com
Brother John	www.brotherjohnf.com

Marc Faber	www.gloomboomdoom.com
Jim Rogers	www.jimrogers.com
Alasdair Macleod	www.financeandeconomics.org/
Michael Krieger	www.libertyblitzkrieg.com
Ann Barnhardt	www.barnhardt.biz
Jeffrey A. Tucker	www.laissezfaire.com
Barry Stuppler	www.minestategold.com
Arch Crawford	www.crawfordperspectives.com
Victor Sperandeo	
Martin Armstrong	www.armstrongeconomics.com
Charles Biderman	www.trimtabs.com
Greg Hunter	www.usawatchdog.com
Dr. Yaron Brook	www.aynrand.org
Val Hughes	www.thevalueguys.com
Mo Mentum	www.thevalueguys.com
Dudley Baker	www.preciousmetalswarrants.com
Peter Degraaf	www.pdegraaf.com
Bob Hoye	www.institutionaladvisors.com/
Turd Ferguson	www.tfmetals.com
David Gurwitz	www.charlesnenner.com
George Matheis	www.moderncombativesystems.net
Rick Rule	www.sprottglobal.com
Ty Andros	www.tedbits.com
James Turk	www.goldmoney.com
Peter Schiff	www.europac.net
Andrew Schiff	www.europac.net
Robert Ian	www.conquerchange.com
David Banister	www.activetradingpartners.com
Gary Wagner	www.thegoldforecast.com
Julian DW Phillips	www.goldforecaster.com
Andrew Horowitz	www.thedisciplinedinvestor.com
Sean T	www.sgtreport.com
Mike Victor	www.thevictoryreport.com
Cliff Ravenscraft	www.thepodcasteranswerman.com
Jason Burack	www.jasonburack.com

And so many hundreds more bloggers and website proprietors that are must reading

Ed Caccia	Listener
"Cyrus"	Listener
Wallace	Listener

And to the thousands of other listeners for helping me make my dreams come true.

Introduction

It's August 2012. The price of gold is closing in on $1700 per ounce and silver's over $30. Last summer it appeared that metal prices were headed to the moon. I myself believed that as the real economy was circling the drain, metals prices were bound to go parabolic. But guess what happened? They peaked and went down instead. And the world is wondering why. And to a lesser extent I am too. Understanding the machinations of the current gold and silver markets requires an understanding of central bank schemes, government money mayhem and the sociopathic tendencies of people who excel in the political sphere. Additionally, understanding precious metals and their relationship to currencies (dollar, euro, pound, etc.) requires a review of the history of money, and money's relationship to gold and silver.

My intent in writing this book is to help make you aware of how precarious the world's current dollar based economic system is and why you need to prepare. Wall Street, the government and central banking have sent our monetary/economic system swan diving into an empty concrete pool, from which there is no escape. Your choice is either to prepare for the coming economic collapse, or to watch the value of all your assets sink to near zero.

You're maybe wondering, who is this guy and what makes him such an expert. I'm probably a lot like you. I grew up in a leafy bedroom community in northern New Jersey. I repeated the Pledge of Allegiance every school day for 13 years. I believed in the American dream. I believed that if you worked hard, played by the rules of the game and persevered, anything was possible. And for a large part of my life, it was, until the crash of 2008 hit and I realized that this time really was different. I heard the call and realized that my life's lessons about economics, human nature, corrupt government and decaying systems were now needed, more than ever.

My father, Nathaniel "Nat" Lutz (1922-1982) was the ultimate teacher about the inherent dishonesty and corrupt nature of government. Born in Elizabeth, New Jersey, his father – Phillip – was then wealthy, by any standard. He singlehandedly developed the modern gas station. Prior to his "groundbreaking" innovation, gasoline was distributed via gravity fed manual pumps. That system worked fine, however, the tanks were elevated at least 10 feet above the surface to provide the force needed to feed the gas through the pump and into a car's tank. Phillip had a better idea. Why not bury the tank and use an electric pump to get it into the gas tank, a revolutionary concept in the early 1900s. They all said it wouldn't work, but of course he proved them wrong. Business took off and he was an overnight success. All was well until 1929, when the first modern age of financial alchemy turned him into a pauper overnight. The rest of his life was an economic struggle, a futile effort to reclaim the success that he had lost.

My father seemed destined to follow in his footsteps. At the young age of 16 he hit a number on the illegal mob run numbers lottery. He used the $1600 in winnings to purchase a beaten down service station. During the Depression it was hard work for very little gain. But my father was optimistic so he gave it a try. He was also a crackerjack mechanic and could strip down a car and rebuild it faster than almost anyone else around. Then World War II started and he reluctantly enlisted in the Army Air Corps. While he was patriotic, his reasons for enlisting in the Air Corps were somewhat selfish. He had visions of trench warfare from WWI and didn't like his chances fighting off artillery shells, mustard gas and snipers. He figured his odds were better flying over the ground troops. And while not much of an athlete, he loved speed, having once gotten a speeding ticket for riding a horse too fast.

He was headed down South to basic training, with his new bride, my mother, Doris, in tow. He hated every minute of officer training school and flight school. There were all sorts of people who just happened to have more stripes on their uniforms telling him what to do. But he knew he had to serve his term. And the Southern food was horrible. While there was a network of Jewish families around the South that gladly took in Northern Jewish GI's, it was a difficult existence, especially for my mother.

Finally the day came when he got his marching orders. Off to India and the Hindu Burma Kush. Two years of eating not much but steamed rice earned him the nickname of "Slim." And I don't mean Slim Pickins, the sociopathic pilot from Dr. Strangelove who eventually rides a nuke into the sunset, or sunrise. Rather, he was six foot one and a half inches and weighed in at 160 pounds.

When he got to India, the Air Corps was offering what looked like a great deal. Fly 1850 hours and you get to go home. Thus the young and naive Second Lieutenant was seen anxiously volunteering for mission after mission, getting very close to the magic number. The flights, while not strictly combat missions, were quite perilous and physically demanding. The Japanese had cut off the overland supply route to China and Dad's job was to safely deliver war materials to the Nationalist and Communist forces that were fighting the Japanese. This was a massive undertaking that involved thousands of airplanes. They traversed the Himalayas, flying right over Mt. Everest (The Hump) in deficient, poorly maintained aircraft. It was extremely dangerous. Over 775 planes crashed in the jungle, killing thousands of troops. 70 years later and they're still recovering those old wrecks from the jungles of India and Burma.

The living conditions were horrible. The only leisure activities were drinking, smoking cigarettes and writing home to loved ones and mail call. But my father, while perhaps not the most enthusiastic gung-ho pilot, did his part. It was 1945 and the war was winding down. At that point, the nature of the cargo he was risking his life to transport changed dramatically. Rather than armaments and war supplies, he was transporting large cans of ketchup and mustard, and crates of feminine hygiene products and condoms. The war had become a corporatist endeavor. Pilots were being forced to risk everything to benefit large American Corporations and their brands. China and India were huge potential markets and what better way to spread the American way of life?

Nat was outraged, as were many of his fellow pilots. Some refused to fly, and were promptly court-martialed and jailed. It was about this time my father had almost flown the requisite hours to necessary to earn a trip home. And then, for no apparent reason, the hours required were increased from 1850 to 2250. He was enraged, but it was only 400 more hours, around 10 missions. So he kept volunteering, closing in on the magical 2250, when they raised it to 2500 hours.

At this point, my father had had enough. While being lied to and deceived by your commanders was not valid grounds for refusing to fly, the captain of the plane could not be forced to fly an un-airworthy craft. So my father would go over every plane with a fine-tooth comb, and if there was a burned out light bulb or a gauge that was acting funky, he would refuse to fly. If he couldn't find anything wrong during the pre-flight inspection, he'd take the plane to the runway and blow out an engine or otherwise sabotage the craft.

The commanders knew exactly what he was doing, they confronted him repeatedly. He insisted that he would fly, "If you get me a plane that's airworthy." This stalemate went on for quite a while and finally they tired of my father's passive-aggressive opposition and sent him home. Thus began my father's lifelong resentment towards and resistance of any governmental authority, whether it was police, elected officials, petty bureaucrats or any other person working under the color of government. He knew from personal experience that the government couldn't be trusted and he refused to accept their authority over him. Yet he continued to vote Democrat because he felt the Republican Party was filled with anti-Semites.

When my father passed away at the young age of 59, there was no question that his stint with the Air Corps was a contributing factor. Flying in unpressurized cockpits over Everest breathing oxygen, caused irreparable damage to his lungs. But smoking and working with asbestos didn't help either.

I inherited my father's distrust of government, the tax system, the monetary system and every other part of it. I'm not an anarchist, but the systems we have in place are starting to make anarchy look acceptable, especially when it comes to the abuse of our rights and the destruction of individual freedom. Resisting the government is in my DNA.

Fast forward to 2012. Since 2007-2008, when the financial crash and collapse began, all we've heard from the government is that the recovery is almost here. Things are getting better. "Happy days are here again." "Prosperity is just around the corner." The exact same line of garbage that the people were fed during the last depression. And it is just as false, misleading and destructive. We need only to look at the real rate of unemployment, nearing 25 percent (see ShadowStats.com). The real inflation rate is over three times the official government rate. The lies never stop. The number of people on food stamps is at 46.5 million. Government never changes its methods. The face of government is all that changes. The lies go on and on.

That is the reason that I'm writing this book. I am on a mission to see that every American is prepared for the ultimate collapse of the dollar and the corrupt worldwide fiat monetary system. It is going to happen. Nothing can stop it. Just as all of Steve Job's billions and the best medical technology in the world couldn't save him, the printing press will not save the dollar, the euro, the yen or the Yuan. And if you accept my premise, this leaves you with a problem. How do you protect the wealth you have left, from the inflationary stealth tax and the eventual collapse of paper money?

One thing is for certain. You absolutely cannot count on Wall Street to secure your future! While there are a number of honest, dedicated, talented investment professionals, they are in complete denial over the collapsing world economy. They see the world through the financial fish bowl and really have trouble thinking outside the box. Very few self-respecting Wall Streeters would ever recommend that you buy physical gold or silver. They would rather put you into fraudulent precious metals ETFs that will become worthless right along with the greenback. There's just not enough income potential for them to ever recommend holding physical precious metals as an investment.

The U.S. went off the last vestige of the gold standard with President Nixon's closure of the gold window in 1971. From that time to now, the average American's standard of living has declined by 57%. Since the midnight chartering of the Federal Reserve in 1913, the dollar has lost over 98% of its purchasing power. These are unalterable facts that the government doesn't want you to know or to think about.

And remember, the U.S. government along with Wall Street jointly created this system that has been destined for the monetary graveyard from the start. Along the way they've made incredible fortunes, which they're currently using to buy gold. Look at it this way. The government created the railroad tracks – the financial system and the fiat dollar. The banks and financial industry created the locomotive, which had no brakes, no reverse gear, with an engine that has to keep going faster and faster. And we, the American public, are all paying the price. And that price is about to get much steeper. While homelessness, tent cities and unemployment have reached pandemic proportions; things are only going to get worse from here.

Capitalism

Capitalism is the fall guy for all of socialism's failings. The system failed. Blame the greedy businessmen. Well, if you're going to blame capitalism shouldn't you know exactly what you're blaming? We constantly hear the word bandied about by commentators, economists and politicians, but they never provide a definition, and most people don't have a clue. Here's one definition that I believe captures the essence of it. "An economic system characterized by the following: 1) private property ownership exists; 2) individuals and companies are allowed to compete for their own economic gain; 3) free market forces determine the prices of goods and services. Such a system is based on the premise of 4) separating the state and business activities; Capitalists believe that markets are efficient; 5) should thus function without interference, and the role of the state is; 6) to regulate and protect only; 7) where absolutely required and no other practical option exists."

Let's deconstruct this definition and see if the U.S. is really has a capitalist economy. 1) An economic system characterized by private property ownership. How much of the United States do local, state and federal governments own? A staggering amount, from office buildings, municipal utilities, dams, auto companies, military bases, national forests, 80 percent of Nevada, thousands of private jets, hundreds of thousands of vehicles and on and on. 2) Individuals are allowed to compete for their own personal gain. Perhaps in some industries, like computers, and various service enterprises. But can anyone seriously believe there's healthy competition in insurance, banks, automobiles, big energy, chemicals, pharmaceuticals, railroads, etc. etc.? Rather, business today is granted certain privileges by government and proceeds to capitalize upon those advantages obtained, to the exclusion of all potential competitors. 3) The tax system favors a GE, which can afford to employ skyscrapers full of tax lawyers and accountants to ensure they pay a zero percent tax rate, unlike their smaller competitors. And without competition between companies, prices never find their optimal level and the company is able to charge its consumers economic rent.

4) No one can seriously argue that big business and the state are separate entities. Government Motors, Government Electric, Government Sachs; the list is inexhaustible. Are the "Too Big to Fail banks" are really independent separate businesses? They were bailed out in 2008, along with hundreds of banks around the globe, courtesy of TARP and the Federal Reserve Bank. The Fed pumped out 16 trillion new currency units to keep the whole game going.

5) When the government is responsible for at least half the economy, then it follows that for many businesses, government will be the biggest customer. As a result, governments are able to call the shots and force such companies to follow policies that are more political in nature, and often diametrically opposed to the best interests of the corporation.

So when you hear whatever the Occupy Movement du jour is ranting about Wall Street and corporatism, while at the same time imploring expansion of the government, look deeper. And while we're on the topic, who's the greatest beneficiary of ever-expanding government and government deficits? Wall Street! So when we say Forget Wall Street, it's not just because they've engaged in an unholy alliance with the government. But rather, the perpetual deficits brought on by ever-expanding government, help increase Wall Street's always-growing profits. Financing the deficit, be it the State of California's, the City of Detroit's or Uncle Sam's, is the major source of Wall Street's profits today. Somebody's got to sell all that debt to unsuspecting suckers/investors. The Fed gives money to these institutions to go buy up that debt in the "Free" Market. And then Wall Street goes out and sells derivatives based on all that newly created debt. So Occupy Wall Street and Wall Street both rely on a constantly expanding government for their health and sustenance.

By now you're starting to grasp the truth about how the economic system works and why you need to prepare for the rapidly approaching day when the system stops working. Read on to learn what real money is, its history and what you can do to protect yourself and your family from the coming financial implosion.

Anyone who claims to know exactly when it will happen is not telling you the truth No one knows the exact timetable. That it will happen is no longer in doubt.

Summary

After reading this book, it is my sincere hope that you will understand the true state of the American and World Economies. They started their final denouement in 2007 and nothing has been done to reverse their ultimate death spiral. The only option an individual has, is to prepare the best that they can. There are too many possible scenarios to prepare for every possible exigency. No one can do that, not even the U.S. government, the UN or China. The system could go down with a whimper, as world leaders get together to hatch a global currency (with an alleged connection to gold). Or it could collapse suddenly, with the death of one or more Too Big to Fail banks bringing on a cascading global crash that stops what is left of the world's economy dead in its tracks. This scenario could possibly lead to massive civil unrest, mass starvation and a "Mad-Max: Beyond Thunderdome" state of being. Or, it could be some where in the middle.

No matter what happens, everyone is in for a major change. The things you thought were solid and beyond reproach, the Federal Reserve, the U.S. government, your retirement financed by Social Security or your private pension, will cease to exist. The extravagant promises made to you by various governmental entities and private corporations, that you'd be set for life and never have to worry about your healthcare, or having money in your pocket, cannot and will not be honored. Understand, they were never intended to be honored in the first place. These promises were the price the government paid to get you to surrender your freedoms and your responsibilities. Their repudiation will be devastating to people all around the globe, in every country in the world. Greece is already suffering this fate. While China and other emerging economies haven't made these types of promises, their economies are often built on export based mercantilist models that will fail just as badly or even worse than the "developed" Western economies.

The choice you're facing is as simple as it is existential. Do you prepare now by purchasing precious metals, building community networks and storing certain of life's essentials? Or do you do nothing and simply wait for the inevitable, hoping against hope that government will somehow pull another rabbit out of the hat and stave off the collapse for another day, week, month, year or decade? The choice is yours and yours alone. In the event that everything turns out just fine, what will it have cost you? Some money invested in metals that will probably go up in price anyway. The essentials you've stored can always be used. So you effectively got paid to purchase insurance and life goes on. But if the scenarios outlined in this book turnout to be correct, and you followed the advice given, you and your family will be safer and more self-sufficient, while the system hopefully reboots, and life at some point returns to normal.

Whatever your decision, good luck and God bless you and those close to you.

Kerry Lutz—August 2012—Greenwich, CT

Gold, Silver and Money

Understanding the current monetary system is essential to your preparations. Key to this understanding is a historical perspective. For thousands of years, gold and silver have always been money. What is money? The dictionary defines money as something that is 1) used as a medium of exchange, 2) a store of value, 3) portable, 4) divisible and 5) relatively scarce.

Societies have used sea shells, rocks, arrow heads and beads as money, but the most enduring forms throughout history have been gold, silver and to a lesser degree copper. Many fiat (government decree with no physical backing) systems have been tried and have always eventually failed.

Gold and silver's history has always been intertwined with the human race's cultural, political, and economic history. Highly valued by many civilizations, regardless of time or place, their relative rarity and beauty, combined with the ease of fabricating them into different shapes and forms, has contributed to their importance, both in the ancient world, and the modern world. Excess wealth has always been used for their purchase.

Many ancient cultures used gold and silver for jewelry and decorative applications, well before their monetary uses evolved. The exact value placed upon them has varied, depending upon the values of the culture involved. For some, such as the Vikings, silver was the more precious metal. In others, like ancient Egypt, gold had a higher value. In more recent times, while the value of gold and silver have fluctuated, being heavily influenced by the discovery of new deposits, gold has steadily remained the more valuable of the two.

During the 20th and early 21st century, gold's value has ranged from 80 to as little as 15 times that of silver. (Known as the silver to gold ratio). As of the writing of this book, silver had recently passed through the crucial 40 to 1 ratio in 2011, but then backed off to its current multiple of 57. But due to the dire state of the world's current monetary system, many experts such as Peter Schiff, Jim Sinclair, David Morgan, Chris Weber and Chris Duane believe silver will appreciate dramatically against gold and all world currencies in the near future.

People have been using gold since at least the 4th millennium BC. Artifacts made from it have been discovered at sites like the Varna Necropolis, a burial site that lies within modern day Bulgaria. Graves there date from 4700 to 4200 BC. The golden artifacts show evidence of sophisticated metallurgy. Other artifacts found in Central European archaeological sites dated back to the 2nd millennium BC. These include the conical headdresses known as golden hats and the Nebra Sky Disk, which is a circle of bronze decorated with shapes representing the moon and stars.

Archaeologists have also found much evidence of ancient silver mining. Slag heaps, waste piles used in silver production, have been found in the Greek islands and in modern day Turkey. Some date back as far as the 4th millennium BC.

Many early civilizations have recorded big gold strikes, but the ancient Egyptians seem to have led the use of this precious metal. Many spectacular burial sites have been filled with golden objects. The volume of gold found in the pyramids and other royal tombs has been shocking. Egyptian hieroglyphic writing dating back to 2600 BC contains numerous references to gold. But, the earliest ancient Egyptian gold reference is a claim by the Mitanni king, Tushratta, that gold was more plentiful than dirt in his country.

Egypt and the nearby country of Nubia, as well as the region across the Red Sea (now part of Saudi Arabia), were all major gold-producing regions during this time. They possessed the required resources and skills to produce large amounts of gold. Remarkably a Nubian gold mine is listed on the earliest known world map, the Turin Papyrus.

Gold and silver cultural references abound, including in ancient religious texts such as the Bible. Many other ancient myths and legends also refer to these precious metals. It has been suggested, that the well-known legend of the Golden Fleece may have its origins in the ancient practice of using a fleece to filter gold particles out of water. The Old Testament contains many references to gold and silver, but the most familiar Biblical reference is in the New Testament, when one of the Magi presents the baby Jesus with a gift of gold; which even at this time was the main symbol of wealth. Silver had a more infamous reference in the Bible, since it was thirty coins of silver that were presented to Judas in return for his betrayal. Silver has also been mentioned in Islam. It has been suggested that the Prophet Muhammad wore a silver ring.

The earliest coins discovered were manufactured around 610 BC. Made from gold in Lydia, which is located in modern day Turkey. Legend has it that gold was exploited in the region since the days of King Midas, who is probably based upon the local 8th millennium BC king, Mita, ruler of the Mushki. In the legend, everything that Midas touched turned to gold, although this blessing soon became a curse when he inadvertently turned his own daughter into a golden statue. Around the same time that coins were being made in Lydia, the Chinese state of Chu was also using square gold coins, known as the Ying Yuan.

The Romans developed large-scale gold production methods when they created hydraulic mining techniques. They were very active in Hispania (the Iberian Peninsula) from about 25 BC and Dacia (in the Carpathian Mountains), from 106 AD. Interestingly, until very recently, gold was still being extracted from opencast mines at the Roman mining site of Roşia Montană in Transylvania. The ruins of a Roman gold mine, together with a modern mine that replaced it, can be found in the U.K. at Dolaucothi.

Silver played a vital part in the growth of Roman Empire. The Romans were able to produce it a scale that was previously unimagined. Their record remained unsurpassed until the discovery of the New World many centuries later. Silver bullion production was one of the major factors that helped stabilize Roman Empire's currency. At the peak, annual silver production hit 200 tons. It is estimated that by the middle of the 2nd century AD, 10,000 tons of silver was circulating in the Roman Empire. This statistic is all the more remarkable when you consider that this represented five to ten times more silver than was present in either medieval Europe or the Islamic Caliphate in 800 AD.

But gold retained its importance long after the fall of the Roman Empire. In the 14th century, it was closely associated with the Mali Empire. In 1324, when the emperor passed through Egypt on his hajj pilgrimage to Mecca, he gave away so much gold to the local people, that the value of gold in Egypt was depressed for the next decade, an early example of metallic monetary inflation. No wonder, half of the Old World's gold in circulation came from Mali. The empire's expansion swallowed up many of the world's most productive gold mines. Amazingly, gold was the coin of the realm.

The medieval world's insatiable thirst for gold led to the specious science of alchemy, which serendipitously became the origin of modern chemistry. The alchemical symbol for gold was a circle with a dot at the centre, which also represented the sun. Silver was represented by the symbol of the crescent moon.

Alchemists tried to find a way to turn other base metals, such as lead, into gold. Had they succeeded, the vastly expanded supply would have made gold just another base metal, thus depriving it of high value. This "blessing" would have been as welcome as the curse of Midas. But medieval man never grasped the economic fundamentals of supply and demand. For the alchemists to have succeeded would have required an understanding of science far greater than was possible at the time. Gold is one of the elements on the periodic table, a basic form of matter. To change one element into another, it must be done at the atomic level. While it is theoretically possible to alter atoms in order to produce gold today, the process is so expensive that this man made gold would cost far more to produce than mining for natural gold.

Silver also played a role in science. Its disinfectant anti-bacterial properties were understood very early. Silver was used to prevent infections in the Classical world and was used in medieval times to preserve food, disinfect water and treat wounds. Silverware, or cutlery also was treasured for its anti-bacterial disease fighting properties. 19th century sailors often placed silver coins in wine and water barrels to kill off harmful microbes that were lurking in these liquids during long journeys.

Gold's use as money has never waned. The desire for gold, silver and other riches was a prime motivator for much of the new world's exploration. As stories of Spain's new found golden wealth reached the rest of Europe, the number of explorers and fortune seekers multiplied. The large amounts of gold that the Conquistadors had taken from South America found its way back to Spain and then across Europe. Metallic monetary inflation occurred once again, as Europe was flooded with metals.

The Aztecs believed gold was the product of the gods, with the literal translation of their name for the metal, teocuitlatl, or god excrement. Many fortunes were made from the theft of riches of the conquered peoples of South and Central America. When this wealth was brought back to Europe, it had significant political consequences. Spain and the Church grew in power from the spoils. This led Britain to back pirates or privateers who attacked Spanish shipping and stole the gold on its way back to Spain.

Throughout much of history most gold was extracted from easy to obtain sources close to the surface. As these readily available sources were depleted, the search was on to go deeper and find harder to recover deposits. Today, most of the world's gold has been extracted from deeper sources. According to estimates, 75 percent of all the gold ever mined, was obtained after 1910. As a side note, if all the gold in the world were brought together in one place, it would equal a 66-foot cube, remarkably small for so large a measure of wealth.

It is important to consider, that while the metals are valuable in their own right, they are also traded as commodities. Therefore, their value can rapidly fluctuate in response supply and demand variances and world economic conditions. When markets perform their price discovery functions properly, their prices will be highest when the supply is limited, and demand is highest. As demand drops or the supply grows, their value should decrease. Over the past 50 years, the world supply of gold has increased greatly. During this time, the supply of silver has and continues to suffer major declines. However, the ability to calculate the exact supply and demand market metrics is a daunting task, which often yields conflicting results, depending upon the analyst's bias.

Gold production rapidly increased during the early 20th century partially as a result of new world discoveries. So many gold rushes took place during the late 19th and early 20th centuries. Fortune seekers would often travel thousands of miles, racing off to the latest rumored gold strike. Upon their arrival, the rumors often proved false or they found fool's gold. This happened in many parts of the world, including the United States, Australia, New Zealand, Brazil, Canada and South Africa.

Major technological breakthroughs greatly increased gold production in the late 1800s that continued throughout the 1900s. Cyanidation extraction, heap leaching, power excavation equipment along with more powerful explosives, enabled lower grade mines to be profitably developed in South Africa and Australia. Miners during the California gold rush could only exploit high quality gold veins. Plucking the low hanging fruit or high-grade near-surface deposits gave way to low-grade ore mining. Many abandoned mines were later re-developed using better technology to extract the deeper lower ore grades. Today miners often develop a property where just a gram of gold or less is present for every ton of rock mined. And with higher prices, miners have begun scavenger hunting, looking through older abandoned mines, as well as searching their own waste piles for gold that can now be economically mined and milled.

Gold and Silver Standards Evolve

Over the last 500 years the two metallic monetary standards were intertwined. Both metals have been used as money for thousands of years. When monetary systems evolved on their own, the people generally chose silver as their money. The supply was greater and since its value was less than gold, it was easier to divide into small denominations. Thus, silver became the money of the common man and gold became the money of the wealthy class. Eventually the gold standard won out over the silver standard and remained dominant, until the U.S.'s adoption of pure fiat money in 1971.

In 1704, The British West Indies was among one of the first world regions to adopt a gold standard. This standard was based on a Spanish gold coin, the doubloon. In 1717, gold began to gain prominence in the UK, when Sir Isaac Newton, who worked for the Royal Mint, altered the mint ratio between silver and gold, essentially creating a gold standard and driving silver out of circulation. The gold standard wasn't official in Britain until 1821, after the creation of the gold sovereign coin. Other countries, including Canada in 1853 and Germany (with the gold mark) the U.S. (with the Eagle) in 1873, soon followed the British into a gold standard, along with the other countries of Britain's Empire. This became known as the Classical Gold Standard.

The United States Constitution provided that the Congress "shall have the power to coin money." In 1792 Congress exercised that authority by passing legislation that provided the production of dollar coins, each to be the value of a Spanish milled dollar, to contain three hundred and seventy-one grains and four-sixteenth parts of a grain of pure, or four hundred and sixteen grains of standard silver. Thus the U.S. started out on a silver standard. However, there was a significant drive for the creation of a bimetallic standard. During the mid 19th century, the U.S. standard had a fixed rate that overvalued silver against gold, which was in demand for trade with England. It was this demand that fueled the California Gold Rush. Silver was coming into the U.S., while gold was leaving the country.

Because the value of gold and silver in the open marketplace vary independently, the production of coins of full intrinsic worth under any ratio will nearly always result in the melting of either all silver coins or all gold coins. In the early 19th century, gold rose in relation to silver, resulting in the removal from commerce of nearly all gold coins, and their subsequent melting. Therefore, in 1834, the 15:1 ratio of silver to gold was changed to a 16:1 ratio by reducing the weight of the nation's gold coinage. This created a new U.S. dollar that was backed by 1.50 g (23.22 grains) of gold. However, the previous dollar had been represented by 1.60 g (24.75 grains) of gold. The result of this revaluation, which was the first-ever devaluation of the U.S. dollar, was that the value in gold of the dollar was reduced by 6%. Moreover, for a time, both gold and silver coins were useful in commerce.

14

In 1853, the weights of U.S. silver coins (except, interestingly, the dollar itself, which was rarely used) were reduced. This had the effect of placing the nation effectively (although not officially) on the gold standard. The retained weight in the dollar coin was a nod to bimetallism, although it had the effect of further driving the silver dollar coin from commerce. Foreign coins, including the Spanish dollar, were also widely used1 as legal tender until 1857.

This undermined confidence in the country's young economy and was a contributing factor in the lead up to the Civil War. After the war started, payments in gold and silver were halted in 1861. The dollar became a fiat currency. At this time the Union also imposed the first income tax, even though it was clearly prohibited by the constitution and later invalidated by the Supreme Court. The Treasury introduced greenbacks to pay for the Union war efforts.

(From Murray Rothbard's What Has Government Done to Our Money?)

The 3 Gold Standards

Classical Versus Exchange

In our exploration of precious metals, their use as money and the evolution of central banking and fiat money, the gold standard in its various forms played a vital role. While not a perfect system, the Classical Gold Standard, upon which the world economic system was base d from 1870 to 1913, in retrospect is seen as an era of unparalleled prosperity and peace.

The use of paper money in America and elsewhere has been a hotbed of discourse for centuries. Most people, be they laymen, economists, or businessmen are often confused and uncertain about what their money is really worth. How did un-backed paper money become the world's medium of exchange? Benjamin Franklin was perhaps the most knowledgeable person in early history on the subject of paper money. He wrote many articles about it.

In colonial times, paper money was a medium of exchange for private trade within the colony or state that issued it. People used paper money to satisfy their financial obligations, such as loan repayments, or taxes owed to the local government that had issued the paper. There was no standardized form of paper money that was accepted between all the colonies or states.

With the Constitutional Convention of 1787, states were prohibited from issuing paper money and monetary matters were the exclusive realm of the federal government. This was the beginning of government charter and regulation of a privately operated banking system. Redeeming paper money was the exclusive obligation of the issuer.

For their notes to be accepted, banks notes had to be 100 percent backed by gold and or silver. Bank notes were to be exchanged on demand at face value. Now that the gold standard is defunct, the Fiat system or Fiat currency derives its value solely from the government's order that it is usable to pay all debts public and private. There is nothing else backing up the system, other than the full faith and credit of the issuing country.

The gold standard in various forms operated from 1821 until 1971. It was a major influence on many industrialized countries' economics policies during this time. In the early years of the twentieth century, the gold standard was arguably the major reason for international financial stability. Gold standard opponents believe that the decades coming after World War I were so injurious and destabilizing of the worldwide economy, because of the world's efforts to re-impose the gold standard. They even claim that it lead up to the worldwide Great Depression.

Three separate forms of the gold standard, classic or gold specie, gold exchange, and gold bullion or Bretton Woods System were used during the last century.

The classic gold standard can be thought of as a bartering system in which gold is used in exchange for another item. The ruling empire determined the value of the gold (or coin). When gold was mixed with other metals, the value decreased. The gold standard gained acceptance as a form of universal money out of acceptance rather than design. Even cultures such as the Byzantine Empire used gold coins. After that empire ended, Europe decided to use silver as its primary currency.

The gold exchange system is a form of finance where silver is used to represent gold. Ruling empires (governments, countries, and so on) are allowed to pass silver coins as currency when they have deposits of gold to back them up. Every government is required to guarantee the value of their coins. Other metals are also used to represent gold, but silver is the metal of standard.

The gold bullion standard came about as a result of international need for global economic exchange rates. The governments buy and sell gold bullion to one another. This established the creation of paper money and bank notes. The Bretton Woods System was the most popular form of the gold bullion standard agreement. This system required world leaders to agree to a price of $35 per ounce.

The gold standard is a financial concept that equates to a country's central bank being responsible to exchange the country's currency for gold when presented for such reason. The exchange rate was determined by the rate at which the national currency was convertible into gold. International debts were all settled in gold.

When a country had a trade surplus, there was an influx of gold into that country's central bank reserves. This in turn meant that the country could increase their money supply as long as they could maintain enough gold to meet any potential demands. This increase of money supply could in turn raise prices nationally, potential reducing exports and raising imports.

With a shortfall of payments, the interest rates would be increased to help balance out the gold flowing out of the national reserves. This in turn would affect lower prices domestically as well as increase exportation and encourage the purchases of local goods over imported goods.

With the fall of the Byzantine Empire, the countries of Europe created the silver standard. The United States adopted the silver standard in the late 1700s and it was thus that trade wars began to drain the coffers of Western Europe and the United States.

It was not until the 1700s, when Sir Isaac Newton was master of the Royal Mint created a new mint ratio between gold and silver, which essentially drove silver out of the market completely. By the 1820s, the United Kingdom was officially on the gold standard, followed in short order by Canada, Newfoundland, the United States, and Germany.

Not until the late 1800s did the United States officially adopt the gold standard (although it had been the de facto standard since 1834), which was led to by a series of financial crises. The famous California Gold Rush of 1849 was a direct result of silver being favored over gold, which of course resulted in the search for more gold. The silver weight of coins was reduced in the early 1850s, and by 1857, the free banking era hit crisis was in full force on an international scale.

Historians claim that this financial crisis was a leading factor in the outbreak of the American Civil War, as the collapse of the international banking system resulted in the United States government disallowing gold and silver payments. The choice to join the ranks of countries who had already adopted the gold standard was an easy one in 1873.

When a country's government wanted to fund projects, such as expensive wars, but did not have the tax revenue to pay for them, they often would go off the gold standard for a brief period of time. For example, when the United States was ensconced in the Civil War, there was a temporary lapse in the exchange of money into gold. As soon as the war concluded, the gold exchange resumed. Britain also suspended their involvement with the gold standard during the Napoleonic Wars.

The result of a country going off the gold standard in order to finance a costly war was most often a staggering economic inflation. Since the individual states were allowed to set their prices at the end of the war, this often resulted in some good being overvalued and some being undervalued. Some states would choose to start back up at pre-war prices, and other did not. This created a system that was unable to deal with the associated arrearages or surpluses.

Although some felt that this problem was a direct result of unionized labor or wage cuts, experts now believe the financial system itself was not solid enough to deal with this financial instability that came about after a period of war as well as all of the technological changes. The beginning of the end was rapidly approaching.

With the First World War, there was another brief suspension in the gold standard. The gold standard effectively suffered from a massive break down during this war as Germany was unable to return to the gold standard since they had lost almost all of their gold reserves to war reparations. In 1914, Germany officially went off the gold standard. Internationally, prices had not been able to right themselves quickly enough, and with the Great Depression, the gold standard died.

The United Kingdom had gone off the gold standard at the beginning of World War I, as did the entire British Empire in exchange for treasury notes instead of gold sovereigns, but the war had effectively bankrupted the country. In 1925, The British Gold Standard Act was brought about to concurrently end the classic gold standard and start the gold bullion standard. This only lasted until 1931, when the UK was forced to suspend this standard as too much gold was being shipped out of reserves.

With the Great Depression in the United States brought heated debate as to the cause of the financial crisis. Some blamed the Federal Reserve and others blamed the gold standard. Both played a part in the problem as the gold standard had the effect of limiting the central banks' policies to expand the supply of money and thereby lower the interest rates. The Federal Reserve could not increase the money supply either, as they were required to maintain 40% backing in gold against the demand notes.

The British recovered much more quickly from the depression than Americans, as they had already abandoned the gold standard several years before. Finally, in 1933, the United States government gave up on the gold standard and the economy started to perk up.

During the Post War era of the mid 1930s to the early 1940s, countries were hesitant to return to a gold standard of international finance. With World War II, countries needed to rebuild financially. The Bretton Woods System or gold exchange standard was adopted to assist struggling countries in this effort. Countries were able to fix their exchange rates relative to the United States dollar. With this agreement, the United States government fixed the price of gold to about $35 per ounce.

Between the years of 1946 to 1971, the United States suffered from balance of payment deficits, which reduced the gold reserves of the United States. Problems were created by such factors as French President de Gaulle reducing their dollar reserves by trading them for gold with the United States. This had the effect of diminishing the United States' financial influence internationally.

The Vietnam War was perhaps the final straw that snapped the back of the gold exchange, as United States President Richard M. Nixon ended the gold exchange in 1971, putting a stop to the direct exchange of dollars to gold. The aftermath of this action is referred to as "Nixon Shock." At the same time, President Nixon imposed a freeze on prices and wages in an effort to stop the rising inflation in the United States.

Nixon Shock is the term used to describe the international sentiment of U. S. President Richard Nixon's decision to abandon the Bretton Woods System with absolutely no international discussion. Since a gold standard's biggest advantage is financial stability, many felt President Nixon's wide affecting decision was quite a selfish move. The U. S. dollar became completely fiat, having no gold backing. The American financial system was thrust back to the 1930s, but didn't even have a link to gold at this point.

There are many advantages to a gold standard system. A gold standard limits the amount of paper money that can be issued by a government. Prices can be inflated when there is an excess of paper money, and fixing the exchange rate on an international basis helps to regulate and stabilize international trade. While there are always imbalances between the prices of objects between countries, the gold standard helps to offset the difference.

With fixed exchange rates, the price levels were affected globally. Balance-of-payment modifications, also called price-specie-flow, allowed prices around the world to stay relatively similar. For example, if a technological advancement is made in the United States, economic growth is brought about. Since the supply of gold is fixed, the prices in the United States will fall. The prices of the exports from the United States will also fall in relation to the price of imports into the United States. This fall in prices of exports will mean that other countries will want our exports. In addition, this will mean the United States will require fewer imports.

A balance-of-payment will be created by this occurrence, which will in turn cause gold to flow from the countries receiving the exports from the United States, into the United States' reserves. This gold influx will increase the United States supply of money, which will in turn reverse that fall in prices that occurred at the start. In addition, the countries that are importing the technology from the United States will reduce their money supply, effectively lowering their prices.

Governmental deficit spending is also reduced by participation in a gold standard system. Governments are unable to hide the actual value of their debts by create use of inflation and the government's central bank cannot be the buyer of last resort of their own debt. With the limited supply of gold, there is no way for a government to create endless, mass quantities of money.

For a gold standard to work effectively, the central banks of all governments involved were expected to play by the rules. This meant that each bank was to raise their discount rate to speed up an influx of gold. The discount rate is the interest rate that a central bank charges on loans to other central banks. This inflow of gold would thereby lower the interest rates. Therefore, if a country was running low on gold they were expected to allow only the outflow to continue until the ration of price level to principal trading was equal to the exchange rate.

The Bank of England was one such central bank that played by the rules quite well. Other countries were not so good at it. France and Belgium for instance, never followed the rules. Neither country ever allowed their interest rates to raise enough to lower their national price levels. Other countries were given to breaking the rules by trading securities in order to guard their national supply of money. In other words, to prevent an inflow of gold, a country would sell securities in exchange for gold, thereby reducing their stores of circulating gold.

The appeal for a gold standard is still strong. Its basic, simple rule is an attractive feature to many who oppose the discretionary powers of the central banks. The anchoring mechanism it has for global prices is another reason some people would prefer a return to the days of a gold standard.

Others oppose a return to the gold standard, as there is no way to provide liquidity to the banks or the markets; gold is not able to expand to meet seasonal growth or demand. Financial emergencies cannot be dealt with, as it cannot grow with an economy. As seen even through the years where a gold standard was in effect, governments had to briefly abandon the standard during times of war.

The solution to these issues was the Federal Reserve System as well as fractional reserve banking. Money is created by the central bank and then is introduced into circulation by spending and the money then expands through the money multiplier. Every loan and redeposit of money expands the base of money.

The global economy relies on the United States dollar as a reserve capital, in which even the price of gold is measured. Many alternative methods have been proposed, but this is so far the method of choice. Several countries hold large reserves of gold as to circumvent the United States dollar. Private stores of gold currency are additional ways of securing wealth.

The Classical Gold Standard

We can look back upon the "classical" gold standard, the Western world of the nineteenth and early twentieth centuries, as the literal and metaphorical Golden Age. With the exception of the troublesome problem of silver, the world was on a gold standard, which meant that each national currency (the dollar, pound, franc, etc.) was merely a name for a certain definite *weight* of gold. The «dollar,» for example, was defined as 1/20 of a gold ounce, the pound sterling as slightly less than 1/4 of a gold ounce, and so on. This meant that the «exchange rates» between the various national currencies were fixed, not because they were arbitrarily controlled by government, but in the same way that *one pound of weight is defined as being equal to sixteen ounces.*

The international gold standard meant that the benefits of having one money medium were extended throughout the world. One of the reasons for the growth and prosperity of the United States has been the fact that we have enjoyed one money throughout the large area of the country. We have had a gold or at least a single dollar standard with the entire country, and did not have to suffer the chaos of each city and county issuing its own money which would then fluctuate with respect to the moneys of all the other cities and counties. The nineteenth century saw the benefits of one money throughout the civilized world. One money facilitated freedom of trade, investment, and travel throughout that trading and monetary area, with the consequent growth of specialization and the international division of labor.

It must be emphasized that gold was not selected arbitrarily by governments to be the monetary standard. Gold had developed for many centuries on the free market as the best money; as the commodity providing the most stable and desirable monetary medium. Above all, the supply and provision of gold was subject only to market forces, and not to the arbitrary printing press of the government.

The international gold standard provided an automatic market mechanism for checking the inflationary potential of government. It also provide an automatic mechanism for keeping the balance of payments of each country in equilibrium. As the philosopher and economist David Hume pointed out in the mid-eighteenth century, if one nation, say France, inflates its supply of paper francs, its prices rise; the increasing incomes in paper francs stimulates imports from abroad, which are also spurred by the fact that prices of imports are now relatively cheaper than prices at home. At the same time, the higher prices at home discourage exports abroad; the result is a deficit in the balance of payments, which must be paid for by foreign countries cashing in francs for gold. The gold outflow means that France must eventually contract its inflated paper francs in order to prevent a loss of all of its gold. If the inflation has taken the form of bank deposits, then the French banks have to contract their loans and deposits in order to avoid bankruptcy as foreigners call upon the French banks to redeem their deposits in gold. The contraction lowers prices at home, and generates an export surplus, thereby reversing the gold outflow, until the price levels are equalized in France and in other countries as well.

It is true that the interventions of governments previous to the nineteenth century weakened the speed of this market mechanism, and allowed for a business cycle of inflation and recession within this gold standard framework. These interventions were particularly: the governments' monopolizing of the mint, legal tender laws, the creation of paper money, and the development of inflationary banking propelled by each of the governments. But while these interventions slowed the adjustments of the market, these adjustments were still in ultimate control of the situation. So while the classical gold standard of the nineteenth century was not perfect, and allowed for relatively minor booms and busts, it still provided us with by far the best monetary order the world has ever known, an order which worked, which kept business cycles from getting out of hand, and which enabled the development of free international trade, exchange, and investment.

After WWI

If the classical gold standard worked so well, why did it break down? It broke down because governments were entrusted with the task of keeping their monetary promises, of seeing to it that pounds, dollars, francs, etc., were always redeemable in gold as they and their controlled banking system had pledged. It was not gold that failed; it was the folly of trusting government to keep its promises. To wage the catastrophic war of World War I, each government had to inflate its own supply of paper and bank currency. So severe was this inflation that it was impossible for the warring governments to keep their pledges, and so they went "off the gold standard," i.e., declared their own bankruptcy, shortly after entering the war. All except the United States, which entered the war late, and did not inflate the supply of dollars enough to endanger redeemability. But, apart from the U.S., the world suffered what some economists now hail as the Nirvana of freely-fluctuating exchange rates (now called "dirty floats") competitive devaluations, warring currency blocks, exchange controls, tariffs and quotas, and the breakdown of international trade and investment. The inflated pounds, francs, marks, etc., depreciated in relation to gold and the dollar; monetary chaos abounded throughout the world.

In those days there were, happily, very few economists to hail this situation as the monetary ideal. It was generally recognized that Phase II was the threshold to international disaster, and politicians and economists looked around for ways to restore the stability and freedom of the classical gold standard.

Fluctuating Fiat Currencies 1931-1945

The world was now back to the monetary chaos of World War I, except that now there seemed to be little hope for a restoration of gold. The international economic order had disintegrated into the chaos clean and dirty floating exchange rates, competing devaluations, exchange controls, and trade barriers; international economic and monetary warfare raged between currencies and currency blocs. International trade and investment came to a virtual standstill; and trade was conducted through barter agreements conducted by governments competing and conflicting with one another.

Secretary of State Cordell Hull repeatedly pointed out that these monetary and economic conflicts of the 1930s were the major cause of World War II.

The United States remained on the gold standard for two years, and then, in 1933-34, went off the classical gold standard in a vain attempt to get out of the depression. American citizens could no longer redeem dollars in gold, and were even prohibited from owning any gold, either here or abroad. But the United States remained, after 1934, on a peculiar new form of gold standard, in which the dollar, now redefined to 1/35 of a gold ounce, was redeemable in gold to foreign governments and central banks. A lingering tie to gold remained. Furthermore, the monetary chaos in Europe led to gold flowing into the only relatively safe monetary haven, the United States.

The chaos and the unbridled economic warfare of the 1930s points up an important lesson: the grievous political flaw (apart from the economic problems) in the Milton Friedman-Chicago School monetary scheme for freely-fluctuating fiat currencies. For what the Friedmanites would do—in the name of the free market—is to cut all ties to gold completely, leave the absolute control of each national currency in the hands of its central government issuing fiat paper as legal tender—and then advise each government to allow its currency to fluctuate freely with respect to all other fiat currencies, as well as to refrain from inflating its currency too outrageously. The grave political flaw is to hand total control of the money supply to the nation-state, and then to hope and expect that the state will refrain from using that power. And since power always tends to be used, including the power to counterfeit legally, the naiveté, as well as the statist nature, of this type of program should be starkly evident. And so, the disastrous experience of Phase IV, the 1930s world of fiat paper and economic warfare, led the U.S. authorities to adopt as their major economic war aim of World War II the restoration of a viable international monetary order, an order on which could be built a renaissance of world trade and the fruits of the international division of labor.

Bretton Woods and the New Gold Exchange Standard 1945-1968

The new international monetary order was conceived and then driven through by the United States at an international monetary conference at Bretton Woods, New Hampshire, in mid-1944, and ratified by the Congress in July, 1945. While the Bretton Woods system worked far better than the disaster of the 1930's, it worked only as another inflationary recrudescence of the gold-exchange standard of the 1920s and—like the 1920s—the system lived only on borrowed time.

The new system was essentially the gold-exchange standard of the 1920s but with the dollar rudely displacing the British pound as one of the "key currencies." Now the dollar, valued at 1/35 of a gold ounce, was to be the only key currency. The other difference from the 1920s was that the dollar was no longer redeemable in gold to American citizens; instead, the 1930's system was continued, with the dollar redeemable in gold only to foreign governments and their central banks. No private individuals, only governments, were to be allowed the privilege of redeeming dollars in the world gold currency.

In the Bretton Woods system, the United States pyramided dollars (in paper money and in bank deposits) on top of gold, in which dollars could be redeemed by foreign governments; while all other governments held dollars as their basic reserve and pyramided their currency on top of dollars. And since the United States began the post-war world with a huge stock of gold (approximately $25 billion) there was plenty of play for pyramiding dollar claims on top of it. Furthermore, the system could "work" for a while because all the world's currencies returned to the new system at their pre-World War II pars, most of which were highly overvalued in terms of their inflated and depreciated currencies. The inflated pound sterling, for example, returned at $4.86, even though it was worth far less than that in terms of purchasing power on the market.

Since the dollar was artificially undervalued and most other currencies overvalued in 1945, the dollar was made scarce, and the world suffered from a so-called dollar shortage, which the American taxpayer was supposed to be obligated to make up by foreign aid. In short, the export surplus enjoyed by the undervalued American dollar was to be partly financed by the hapless American taxpayer in the form of foreign aid.

There being plenty of room for inflation before retribution could set in, the United States government embarked on its post-war policy of continual monetary inflation, a policy it has pursued merrily ever since. By the early 1950s, the continuing American inflation began to turn the tide the international trade. For while the U.S. was inflating and expanding money and credit, the major European governments, many of them influenced by "Austrian" monetary advisers, pursued a relatively "hard money" policy (e.g., West Germany, Switzerland, France, Italy). Steeply inflationist Britain was compelled by its outflow of dollars to devalue the pound to more realistic levels (for a while it was approximately $2.40). All this, combined with the *increasing productivity of Europe, and later Japan, led to continuing balance of payments deficits with the United States. As the 1950s and 1960s wore on, the U.S. became more and more inflationist, both absolutely and relatively to Japan and Western Europe. But the classical gold standard check on inflation—especially American inflation—was gone. For the rules of the Bretton Woods game provided that the West European countries had to keep piling upon their reserve, and even use these dollars as a base to inflate their own currency and credit.*

But as the 1950s and 1960s continued, the harder-money countries of West Europe (and Japan) became restless at being forced to pile up dollars that were now increasingly overvalued instead of undervalued. As the purchasing power and hence the true value of dollars fell, they became increasingly unwanted by foreign governments. But they were locked into a system that was more and more of a nightmare. The American reaction to the European complaints, headed by France and DeGaulle's major monetary adviser, the classical gold-standard economist Jacques Rueff, was merely scorn and brusque dismissal. American politicians and economists simply declared that Europe was forced to use the dollar as its currency, that it could do nothing about its growing problems, and that therefore the U.S. could keep blithely inflating while pursuing a policy of "benign neglect" toward the international monetary consequences of its own actions.

But Europe did have the legal option of redeeming dollars in gold at $35 an ounce. And as the dollar became increasingly overvalued in terms of hard money currencies and gold, European governments began more and more to exercise that option. The gold standard check was coming into use; hence gold flowed steadily out of the U.S. for two decades after the early 1950s, until the U.S. gold stock dwindled over this period from over $20 billion to $9 billion. As dollars kept inflating upon a dwindling gold base, how could the U.S. keep redeeming foreign dollars in gold—the cornerstone of the Bretton Woods system? These problems did not slow down continued U.S. inflation of dollars and prices, or the U.S. policy of "benign neglect," which resulted by the late 1960s in an accelerated pileup of no less than $80 billion in unwanted dollars in Europe (known as Eurodollars). To try to stop European redemption of dollars into gold, the U.S. exerted intense political pressure on the European governments, similar but on a far larger scale to the British cajoling of France not to redeem its heavy sterling balances until 1931. But economic law has a way, at long last, of catching up with governments, and this is what happened to the inflation-happy U.S. government by the end of the 1960s. The gold exchange system of Bretton Woods—hailed by the U.S.

*political and economic Establishment as permanent and impregnable—began
to unravel rapidly in 1968.*

Abandonment of the gold standard was the natural result of central
banking's ascendancy. Today, there is no country on the gold standard. The
fiat money system that took its place has been dominated by the U.S. dollar,
the world's reserve currency since WWII. The dollar has been steadily devalued ever since the chartering of the Federal Reserve in 1913. The result
has been trade imbalances, with certain countries holding ever-increasing
amounts of the U.S.'s depreciating currency. Until the world financial collapse of 2008, there was little interest in, or discussion about, returning to a
gold or precious metal monetary standard.

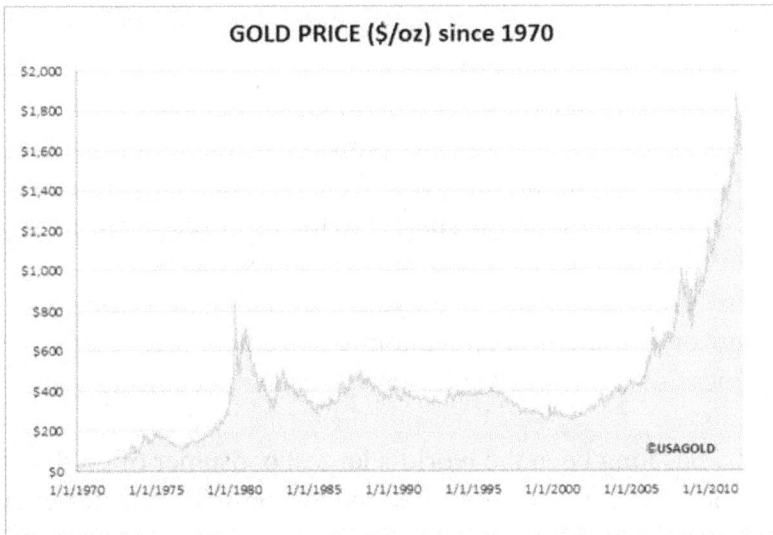
GOLD PRICE ($/oz) since 1970

Economists justify abandonment of precious metal-backed currencies, with their claim that economic growth would be limited by the amount
of gold and silver available. The dwindling supply would thus limit the
amount of currency in circulation, which would limit growth. Modern economists cannot accept a monetary system where the value of the currency
unit can actually appreciate over time. The idea that consumer-purchasing
power can increase is anathema to the banks. An appreciating currency
would lessen their profits and make repayment extremely difficult during
recessions and depressions. When it comes to banking, there's nothing more
profitable and safe than fiat currency, allowing them to create money and
resulting profits out of thin air.

In the late 20th and early 21st centuries, the value of gold has increased dramatically, from $20 per ounce in 1932 to over $1700 per ounce as of this writing. Gold has retained and increased its value, because of its use in computer chips, jewelry and most importantly, investment demand. Its value has been increasing at a faster pace than almost any other time in history. Due to the severity of the financial crisis, some investors have turned to gold which they believe it is a more stable store of value. Savvy successful men such as Jim Rogers, Jim Sinclair and Dr. Marc Faber argue that in light of the inherent long-term instability of fiat currencies, gold and silver are becoming re-monetized and will again resume their rightful place as the "King and Queen of currencies."

In addition, central banks around the world have rediscovered this most "barbarous" of relics. China, India, Russia, Korea, Thailand, Kazakhstan, Mexico and many others have increased their reserves over the past few years. Now the Bank for International Settlements (BIS), a kind of Central Bank of Central Banks, has passed rules giving gold preferential treatment in determining private banks' capital adequacy. In response, the Federal Reserve has brought the subject to the forefront in requests for comments about treating gold as cash reserves in U.S. banks.

Many important financial players are coming to see gold as an indispensible part of a stable global economic system. A recent survey showed that 90 percent of all hedge fund managers were acquiring gold for their own accounts.

India has long been the world's largest consumer of gold, ostensibly for the payment of dowries, which can range from 30 grams to several kilos in the case of wealthier brides. Indian jewelry is 22 carat gold, and is really just an ornamental investment. China, which had banned gold and silver ownership for decades, not only legalized its purchase, but has been waging a campaign to encourage citizens to stock up. Only in the United States and Europe does it appear that gold demand has not escalated. While demand has increased from the anemic levels of the 1980's and 1990's, citizens of these areas have been told for many years that paper assets have value and that in the words of the late John Meynard Keynes, "Gold is nothing more than a barbarous relic."

For the past hundred years, the system appeared to operate well, if you ignore the frequent breakdowns and revaluations and tinkering needed to keep it functioning. At the present time, **just 1-2 percent of the world's wealth is held in precious metals**! King Midas must be rolling in his grave.

Paper Money–Print and Pray

The Chinese invented paper money in the 1100s. Marco Polo, on visiting China, believed that paper money was among the greatest inventions he ever witnessed, until he experienced hyperinflation. Rather than an incredible invention, the Chinese then referred to paper money as "flying money." No sooner did you get it in your hands, than it flew out!

Paper money, bills or banknotes are, in essence, promissory notes issued by banks and used as a medium of exchange, or money. Base metal (copper, zinc, nickel) coins and banknotes make up all of the cash money that is used in the world today. There are non-circulating coins that have particularly high values, such as the U.S. Silver Eagle and U.S. Gold Eagle. But these coins are produced for collectors and investors and are never used in commerce.

Always remember that the cost of producing coins and banknotes is far lower than their monetary value. This is why silver was removed from U.S. coins in 1965. The metal value was becoming greater than the face value. This happened with the copper penny in 1982 and will eventually happen to the current nickel. The profit that governments/central banks realize creating money (face value of new currency minus the cost of production) is called seigniorage. If you've ever wondered why counterfeiting is so intensely prosecuted, monetary production is left to the Treasury and central banks and they do not appreciate any competition.

Throughout history, many different types of materials have been used to create currency. Bartering systems evolved in communities in order to facilitate trade of goods and foster production of necessary items. Among the oldest forms of money, were goods such as cattle and grain. Later systems evolved that used objects like cowrie shells as a form of currency. Eventually metal coins were created to provide a portable, easily recognizable and efficient form of money. However, much of the money that is used in the world today is in the form of digital currency. It has no physical reality, other than being born into being by either the government or a private borrower, borrowing it into existence. The U.S. and the world have created debt-based currencies. (See below)

While paper currency is today ubiquitous, its invention required a major paradigm shift in the way that money was viewed. Most of the earlier currencies were precious metals based coins. Their metallic value equaled their face value, and the seigniorage only consisted of the cost of fabricating gold and silver into coins. Banknotes, which are printed on paper, possess no intrinsic value, so in order to use them as money, both the buyer and the seller must be able to agree on their value. Today this agreement is forced upon the parties by governments' imposition of legal tender laws, which require citizens and businesses to accept the notes in satisfaction of payment of all debts both private and public.

Paper money has many advantages over traditional metal coins. While the paper itself does not have value, due to governmental edict or fiat, these notes until faith in them is lost, have value. Of course they are more portable, easier to carry and hide and can represent almost any value that the mint ascribes to them.

The history of paper money involves the use of two different forms. Drafts are the first type of paper money and they were also the earliest form. They are receipts that represent value, which is held on account. A farmer could be issued a draft on the basis of their expected future agricultural produce, such as their yield of capital or grain. Drafts could also be issued on the basis of stores of grain.

Bills are the second type of paper money. A bill is a paper banknote that has been issued with a promise from the issuer to convert it at a later date. Banknotes were originally seen simply as promissory notes. They had no intrinsic value of their own, but they did represent a certain amount of something valuable such as gold. The banknote was essentially an I.O.U. with a promise to pay the amount in gold. As gold and silver standards ceased to be used, bills came to represent credit money or fiat money, which is a term for credit backed by the government.

The first banknotes in the world were not actually made out of paper. In China, around 118 BC, a form of banknote was created that was made out of leather. These banknotes were about a foot square and they were printed with colored borders. Although not made from paper, they were used in the same way as paper money.

China also has the dubious distinction of being the first to use actual paper in the creation of money. The earliest paper banknotes are believed to have originated there around 806 A.D. Paper money was used in China for the next 500 years, from the 9th century until the 15th century.

The first paper money in China was created during the Sung Dynasty. It was only used in certain parts of the country and it was not a national currency. Only small amounts were produced, and each paper note had an expiration date. All of the banknotes were to be replaced every three years, according to government regulations. The person who held the banknote would have to pay a three percent charge in order to exchange their old expired banknote for a new one. However, in practice, the banknotes were never retired, although new banknotes were constantly being produced. And of course by 1106, this led to serious inflation, as more and more banknotes were in circulation.

Under the Yuan Dynasty, the expiration dates for the banknotes were abolished. This allowed the paper banknotes to match the rates of hard commodities such as silver, gold and silk. The Yuan dynasty actually abolished the use of metal coins and required people to pay their taxes in paper money, an example of an early legal tender law. Despite these changes made by the Yuan Dynasty, inflation continued in China, as a result of wars within the country. The currency suffered an inflationary collapse in 1455. Learning their lesson, paper money ceased to be in use in China, during the time of the Ming Dynasty.

Inflation has been a nagging problem ever since. Every subsequent attempt to perfect paper money has led to the exact same result, collapse. Having learned their lesson, the Chinese didn't use paper money for several hundreds of years. While paper money was falling out of use in China, Europe had yet to develop its own form of paper currency. It would be another three hundred years before banknotes and paper currency would be considered commonplace.

Venetian merchants, upon hearing about the state-backed paper money of China, were duly impressed. The only notes then in use in Europe were those issued by private bankers or merchants. Banknotes (actually a promissory note) were exchanged in Europe from the 14th century on, but they were not first accepted as currency. A banknote would be issued to an individual, as a receipt for the deposit of a certain amount of gold or silver, entrusted to the care of the banker. The paper money was actually backed by the real wealth of the depositor. Anyone holding this paper note would be able to collect the gold or silver from the bank. The note could be exchanged between different people and used to make purchases. Each note was created individually for the holder rather than being a standard note that was produced in large amounts.

Notes of the bank or nota di banco were used across Europe in the 14th century, as well as in Italian merchant colonies outside of Europe. When payments were to be made internationally, they were often made with bills of exchange or lettera di cambio, rather than with notes of the bank. Lettera di cambio were promissory notes that were based on virtual currencies, rather than on physical currencies that were still in use. A virtual currency was usually a type of coin that was no longer actually used, but which could be considered a standard since all current physical currencies were based upon it. These virtual currencies could therefore be traded in note form internationally, as it would be clear how much the note represented in the currencies of the different countries.

Banknotes that more resembled modern paper money were first used in Flanders and Italy, during the middle ages. Money traders used promissory notes to effectively transport money over long distances, when transporting gold or silver would be unsafe. The earliest promissory notes were registered to the individual to whom they were issued, much like a modern check, but later came to resemble modern banknotes, since promised amount would be payable to whomever held the note (the bearer).

It was the Stockholm's Banco of Sweden that issued the first true European paper money in 1660. However, people still desired the perceived security of coins, which the banknotes were payable in, and the bank experienced problems due to loss of confidence. In 1664, it ran out of coins to issue to holders of its banknotes and it had to cease operations. Thus the modern bank run was born.

The Bank of Scotland was chartered in 1695. It started as a private bank and dealt with only the wealthiest clients, taking deposits and making commercial loans. It issued 5, 10, 20, 50 and 100 shilling banknotes. Their notes looked more like checks than modern currency. Scotland was also the first country to use color in its banknotes, which it began to do in 1777.

In the English Colonies, paper money became a necessity, as England demanded the export of the colonies' precious metal based money. The Massachusetts Bay Colony in 1690 was the first issuer of paper money. The other colonies were quick to issue their own paper money and inflation was quick to follow, with the exception of Pennsylvania, that somehow managed a more responsible policy.

In the aftermath of the French and Indian Wars, Britain's was heavily in debt and wanted more control over colonial monetary policy to pay off their debts. In 1751, Parliament had forbidden the New England colonies from making their currency legal tender. British Banks and creditors were still nervous about accepting Colonial currency for any debts, as they lacked confidence in its value. Therefore, to help mollify them, in 1764, Parliament passed the Currency Act, which extended the ban of paper money as legal tender to all the colonies.

The result was a decline in the value of existing paper money, since nobody was obligated to accept it in payment of debts, even in the colonies. There were no gold and silver mines in the colonies so the Currency Act had a deflationary impact upon the money colonial money supply. This combined with new duties and stricter enforcement, delivered a severe shock to a colonial economy already suffering a postwar business decline. The colonists were caught between a rock and hard place. And this became one of the major grievances leading to the Revolutionary war.

Finally, in 1775 the US got a "national" paper currency compliments of the Continental Congress. During the 18th century, the thirteen colonies had at various times each issued their own banknotes. The new paper currency "the Continental" had a much wider reach. It was created to help pay the Revolutionary War's enormous costs. It was to be backed with the future tax revenues that the Congress expected to raise, as there wasn't gold or silver available to back it. Counterfeiting of the Continentals was serious and helped lead to significant currency depreciation. Inflation was so great and confidence so low, that the phrase, "Not worth a continental," became embedded in the young nation's lexicon.

Alexander Hamilton, the first Secretary of the Treasury, was extremely concerned about the United States' credit worthiness. He believed that if the financial system was not quickly shored up and creditors paid off, the country would collapse. Heroic soldiers had been unpaid for years and many of the newly formed northern states were mired in war debts. He believed that keeping the country secure and stable required the federalization of all war debts and the formation of a national bank.

It appears his intentions were good, if not short sighted. His plan for the bank would make it private, prevent foreign control, forbid it from buying government debt and stop it from printing money beyond it's actual capital. In addition, his proposed excise tax on whiskey to finance the new republic, led to the Whiskey Rebellion. (Something that continued on until Prohibition)

Jefferson and Madison opposed the bank, but it eventually passed the house and the senate and in 1791 and became law. Its twenty-year charter expired in 1811. The first era of American central banking and paper currency began. The first of its major responsibilities was to issue standard banknotes to simplify the currency, reduce the confusion and make trading easier.

During the Civil war, Congress authorized the treasury to print paper money in the form of demand notes in 1861, later known as Greenbacks. the notes did not carry a promise of interest, but their use enabled the government to raise funds, which it needed in order to pay for the cost of the Civil War. During this time, the US had a defacto fiat currency. From 1865 and 1933, gold certificates that were based on deposits of gold bullion were used in the U.S. the U.S. treasury did all of the engraving and printing involved in the production of paper money in the U.S.. Politicians want avoid huge taxes increases, so they invariably choose the easier route, which is to inflate the currency. Greenbacks were introduced into circulation by the treasury to pay costs of the Union.

One difference between a Civil War Greenback and the notes currently in use, is that the original 1861-1862 were actually considered Demand Notes.

Banknotes in Europe continued to be issued by small creditors for local circulation rather than by the state for national circulation, until the reign of Louis XIV in early 18th century. It was at this time that state-backed paper money was created for use as currency in France, thanks to the economist John Law. While printing additional paper money was initially thought to be an easy route to increasing the country's wealth and output, the French found out within several years that true wealth is never created by the printing press. Once Pandora's printing press was started, it proved impossible to stop. The presses worked 18 hours per day producing fresh bank notes. Hyperinflation was the end result, eventually leading to the French Revolution and the rise of Napoleon.

On taking power, the first thing Napoleon did was to stabilize the currency by implementing a bi-metallic standard. Amazingly, while engaged in The Napoleonic Wars, Britain was forced off the gold standard and endured sustained inflation, while France remained on a bimetallic standard for the war's duration. For wars of comparable length and intensity in the nineteenth and twentieth centuries, Napoleonic war finance stands out. It was the last time a war was paid for in gold. As a side note, the proceeds of the Louisiana Purchase went to war finance.

During the 19th century paper money's convenience became increasingly popular. A number of countries looked to paper as a replacement for their coin based currencies. Often this was due to conflict or regime changes. And politicians can seldom resist the attractions of paper. The urge to inflate and promise more to the people than can possibly be delivered in an honest monetary system eventually won out. However, from this time until the beginning of World War I, the classical gold standard was generally well adhered to which kept the paper currency relatively honest.

With the adoption of the Gold Standard by England in 1816, British banknotes became linked directly to the value of gold. The banknotes used in England prior to this were not directly tied to any standard, although paper money had long been used in Europe. Following the establishment of the gold standard, each English banknote represented a specific amount of gold. This enabled the production of standardized non-inflationary paper money.

Germany began to use paper money in 1873. It named its new paper currency the gold mark since it was based on the gold standard. In 1914, however, the connection between Germany's paper currency and the gold standard was lost during the economic upheavals associated with the First World War. After 1914 the currency in Germany became known as the papiermark. The papiermark was replaced by the reichsmark in 1924, following problems with rising inflation. A single reichsmark was worth a trillion papiermarks. This huge difference necessitated the need for the rentenmark, an intermediate currency that was based on the gold standard. Germany's currency changed again in 1948, becoming the Deutsche mark in West Germany, a currency that was issued by the U.S., the UK and France. The Deutsche mark replaced both the reichsmark and the rentenmark. The Deutsche mark would later bring East and West Germany back together following the collapse of the Soviet Union.

Japan's Meiji government was the first to establish a generally accepted paper currency in the country, in 1872. This currency was named the yen. It too was based on the gold standard. The earliest yen banknotes had a design that was based upon that of the U.S. dollar banknotes. The Japanese yen was linked to the U.S. dollar from the end of the First World War up until 1973.

China returned to the use of paper money during the 1890s, having forgotten the lessons of its earlier paper money experiment hundreds of years earlier. The new paper money was based upon the existing Chinese currency, the Yuan. The Yuan was itself based upon the silver standard. Banknotes were issued through the Chinese banks, which meant that by the 1930s, there were a number of different types of paper banknotes circulating throughout the country. This situation was exacerbated by the introduction of Japanese money into the country following their invasion that decade. In 1948 the currency was switched back to the gold standard.

Although national, state-backed paper currencies are still the norm in the world today, there are some exceptions. The Euro, for example, is an international currency used across Europe. In some parts of the world, private banknotes are still used. For example, in the United Kingdom, some commercial banks in Scotland and Northern Ireland continue to produce their own banknotes, which are commonly used in their regional areas, although they are not considered legal tender. Banknotes issued by the Bank of England are used throughout the UK, but they are only considered legal tender in England and Wales. And in Hong Kong, the currency is issued by a number of commercial banks, the Bank of China and the Hong Kong Monetary Authority.

Modern banknotes are usually made from cotton paper, which has a weight of between 80 and 90 grams per square meter. Other fibers such as linen may be mixed in with the cotton. Cotton paper is tougher and more resilient than normal paper, so it is a better choice for banknotes. The average banknote is expected to remain in circulation for about two years. In Japan, banknotes are printed on paper produced from the bark of the mulberry tree. This is the same material that was used to make early banknotes in China. Polymer banknotes are used in some countries, such as Australia and Canada. Despite looking similar to paper money, these banknotes are made using plastics. Banknotes are usually made in molds, with watermarks and threads being incorporated as the paper forms. These are some of the security devices used to help prevent counterfeiting.

It has been suggested that, just as paper money has replaced metal coins and precious metals, it may itself be replaced in the future by the use of electronic currencies. More and more transactions take place electronically, online and with credit and debit cards. The world's governments have warmed to the idea of eliminating physical currency, as it makes it easier to spy on citizens and track transactions, thus making it harder to avoid taxes or engage in illegal forms of commerce.

Sweden appears may be the first country to achieve a truly "cashless" society. As of now, cash is used in less than three percent of all transactions within the country. Obviously, black markets will continue as they have in the past. As long as people want things that are prohibited by the government, man will find a way to provide those items. And people will not be writing to checks or using debit or credit cards to obtain them. Whether its gold, silver or another country's currency, illegal commerce will continue 'til the end of time.

Central Banking

What is a central bank? It is an institution that issues and manages a state's currency, money supply, interest rates and perhaps the country's supply of gold bullion. This right to issue currency is a monopoly granted by the state as a condition of the central bank's charter. The rise of central banking occurred early in the evolution of the modern economic system. As economies expanded, so did trade between countries as well as the financial needs of businesses and individuals. It became necessary to devise systems to facilitate both domestic and foreign commerce. Expanding government operations required financing and the ability to raise capital to fund the state. Wars were frequent costly endeavors of the ruling elite.

Early central banks were usually private institutions, granted franchises by each particular country. Once their responsibilities increased to include currency issuance, then money supply regulation became necessary to insure economic stability. Controlling and manipulating interest rates became the primary tool to further this end. In some countries, such as the U.S., the central bank also became the prime overseer of the commercial banking system.

Modern Central Banking

Central banks, unlike their commercial brethren, create and maintain a country's currency. The currency produced by the central bank is almost always the country's legal tender. Although the central bank may also have other functions, it is the production of currency that is typically the main role of a central bank.

Most modern central banking is based upon the premise of political and governmental independence. This theory holds that isolation from political pressure and interference will lead to better functioning, more stable economies. However, the premise has proven flawed, as central banks do not exist in a vacuum and their continuity is dependent upon the interdependence of close governmental relationships.

The modern world's monetary evolution has come about as the result of central banking. What we call and use as money is the direct product of central banking, which is the result of governments legally defining the monetary units to be used in conducting trade within an economy. Prior to the 17th century, money in circulation was often the product of private banks, agreements by private parties, and the product of both public and private mints. Its creation and use was quite limited because it usually was backed by either gold or silver. Systemic monetary problems occurred when countries slipped off metallic standards.

Most pre-17th century currency was commodity money; its value was derived from the commodity from which it was made. Promises to pay (notes) were used 500 years before this time, in Asia and in Europe. Paper money was also used regionally in many parts of the world. Newly formed central banks initially adhered to a metallic standard, where notes were freely converted into gold or silver. But a distinct pattern has evolved where convertibility has ended in favor of a purely fiat unit. At the present time the world is on a fiat money standard. Fiat money as the saying goes, "Isn't worth the paper it's printed upon."

Today, people around the world take money for granted and have no concept of its evolution or its intrinsic value. But the Merriam-Webster Dictionary's definition tells us all we need to know. Fiat: 1) a command or act of will that creates something without or as if without further effort; 2) an authoritative determination; and 3) an authoritative or arbitrary order. So fiat money derives its value from government edict or order. It is authoritarian by nature and reading between the lines, we see that it forces people to do something that they might not ordinarily be disposed to do of their own free will.

Legal Tender Laws

Of course the mere decree that an otherwise worthless pieces of paper in and of itself has value, would not be enough to force an informed and free populace to start using it for trade and transactions, or as a medium of exchange and a store of value. Another compulsory edict was required to force public compliance: Legal Tender Laws. The term "legal tender" evolved from Middle English tendren, French tendre (verb form), meaning to offer. The Latin root is tendere (to stretch out), and the sense of tender as an offer is related to the etymology of the English word extend (to hold outward). The noun form of a tender as an offering is a back-formation of the noun from the verb. Legal tender is a medium of payment, mandated by law or imposed by the legal system. It insures that a currency is valid for meeting financial obligations, both public and private. Paper/digital currency is the accepted form of legal tender in all countries today.

In the 17th century, before central banking, the Knights Templar played a similar role Europe. The promises-to-pay issued by the Knights Templar were highly respected and they became akin to modern currency. A person could give the Knights cash for safe keeping in Europe, receive a receipt and then cash it in at another Templar outpost in the Middle East. The Knights Templar's activities actually formed the basis of the modern banking system. The Bank of Amsterdam, created in 1609, was another step towards central banking. It was the first public bank to offer accounts that were not directly convertible to coins.

Sweden founded the world's first central bank, known as the Riksbanken or the Sveriges Riksbank. Opened in 1664, it still operates today. As a joint stock bank its purpose was to lend directly to the Swedish government.

Before the Bank of England, the British used a system known as the tally stick. Tally sticks were matching pairs of wooden sticks that acted as receipts for transactions between two parties. The sticks were originally joined together. A series of notches would be cut across them to mark a loan or other financial transaction. Then, the tally sticks would be spilt down the middle, creating two matching tally sticks with identical notches that would fit together exactly. Each party involved in the transaction kept one of the sticks. The monarchy used them and accepted them for payment of taxes. This system was used alongside other forms of currency, for more than 700 years. However, Bank of England's formation in 1694 meant the tally system's days were numbered. While the Bank's founders used tally sticks to buy their shares, they then turned around and ended the tally stick system. The Bank took complete charge of British currency, prohibiting any competing currencies from ever being used.

William Paterson founded the Bank in the part of London known as "The City". As a joint stock company, its main purpose was to manage government debt and to finance the all too numerous wars of England. Its role today has been greatly expanded, with economic stability and control of inflation at the top of the list. However, growth, economic stability and controlling inflation are tasks so gargantuan that no group of bankers, in

Britain, China, Japan or the U.S. are capable of handling it. There are too many factors that affect the billions of transactions that people around the world enter into daily. The belief that a group of elitist bankers have a somehow better vantage point for planning out and controlling the world economy is absurd.

While central banks have been formed for numerous reasons, dealing with and solving serious economic crises is often top of the list. 1800 Napoleon established the Banque de France, to help to stabilize the currency, which had suffered hyperinflation which led to the French revolution. Its first priority was to stabilize the country by stabilizing the currency. This meant a move back to the gold standard. Inflation ceased to be a concern and Napoleon was hailed a hero.

Early central banks, while providing important support for governments, also acted as private banks in their own right. Central banks became clearinghouses for individual promissory notes, private bank notes and handled many other commercial transactions. The private banking sector came to rely upon them to clear notes from other states and countries. This function evolved in the normal course of business. A central bank would wind up holding notes from many other banks, both domestic and foreign. This historic relationship, helped form the current partnership of private and central banks. And of course, central banks could always be an important source of credit, as the lender of last resort for any financial institution that was having difficulty meeting deposit demands.

War finance has always been a vital central bank task and many argue a major reason for their existence. As a nation's war debt increased, central banks could always be counted on to purchase more debt, especially when private parties refused to. This is exactly why the Bank of England was chartered. King William III was at war with France. He was short on funds to keep the hostilities going. Rather than seek peace, he engaged a syndicate of City traders and merchants to underwrite a £1.2m issuance of government debt. In exchange, they received a charter, which included many privileges such as authority to issue notes (print money). This syndicate soon evolved into the Bank of England, financing numerous wars for the Duke of Marlborough, and later Imperial conquests by Charles Montagu, 1st Earl of Halifax like the Seven Years War and many subsequent conflicts. The British National Debt owed to the Bank of England increased substantially during each period of warfare, up to and including the First World War. After the Second World War, the Bank was nationalized.

An example of why the Bank of England became so essential can be seen in the causes of the English Civil War. Lacking a central bank, the King increased taxes to unreasonable levels to keep fighting. The English Civil War and revolution beginning in 1642 was financed by money lenders who made large profits as the King and the supporters of Oliver Cromwell and the Parliament fought one another during 50 years of expensive turmoil. The profits made at this time enabled the bankers to take over the City of London, creating the economic center of the United Kingdom and the world

No discussion of central banking is complete without examining The Rothschild family's key role in the acceptance and expansion of central banking. The name Rothschild originated from the name of a German gold-smith's shop, the Red Shield Firm, set up in 1743 by Amshall Moses Bower. The family later changed their name to Rothschild, which means "Red Shield." The business started by making individual loans, but soon found that lending to royalty and governments was far more profitable. Along with bigger loans came bigger profits. The debt was secured by their clients' collection of public taxes. The Rothschild family quickly spread its business throughout Europe, with the practice of sending its sons to important cities around the world, to set up their own bank branches. The Rothschild family played a key role in the creation of central banks in many countries. Through their control of the banking system, they became the richest and most powerful family in Europe and perhaps the world.

Struggling to cope with this taxation during a time when there was a shortage of materials for producing coins in America, the colonies created their own paper money, called Colonial Script. This was a form of paper money produced by the colonies for use in the colonies. It helped to encourage local trade, it was not backed by a gold or silver standard, and it freed the colonies from the Bank of England.

The Bank of England was unhappy with this state of affairs, so it used its influence on the British government to press for the passage of the 1764 Currency Act. This act made it illegal for the colonies to issue their own currencies and it forced them to pay all of their taxes to the British government in gold or silver. As a result, the American colonies slid into an economic depression. This was a significant factor in the Revolutionary War, which led to the end of British rule.

In France, Napoleon was naturally suspicious of central banking. His reticence to borrow from the central bank led to the Louisiana Purchase in 1803. The three million dollars in gold the U.S. paid him went to fund his European wars. His opponents' major source of funding was the Bank of England. Had Napoleon been victorious, the British central bank would have collapsed.

Unlike the earlier central banks, which were often created to meet the borrowing needs of governments, the Federal Reserve and other central banks created around the same time were established in order to consolidate the financial system and to provide stability.

The central banks that developed in Europe and Japan during the 19th and 20th centuries used the international gold standard. However, free banking and currency boards were used elsewhere. Economic problems around the world during these two centuries were used to build the case for central banks, especially in those countries that were still relying on the older "outdated" banking systems. Whenever and wherever an economic crisis struck, banks would collapse. Countries such as Australia, which did not have a central bank, were beginning to see the need for a more stable central banking system.

After the First World War, the role of central banking in economic stability became more accepted and urgent. Central banking spread quickly around the world. Not coincidentally, the rise of central banking happened at the same time the gold standard was collapsing. Since currencies were no longer completely linked to the value of gold, central banking systems and fiat money became more and more prevalent.

Congress created the U.S. Federal Reserve in 1913. The first Australian central bank arrived in 1920, with Canada following suit in 1923, Mexico and Chile creating theirs in 1925, and New Zealand joined the ranks in 1934. By 1935 Brazil was the only significant world economic power without one. It developed a precursor in 1945, but didn't get one for another twenty years. Newly independent Asian and African countries who had recently broken free of their colonial masters quickly formed their own central banks.

China began to develop a central bank in 1979, known as the People's Bank of China. However, it wasn't until 2000 that the People's Bank morphed into a modern central bank, with powers and responsibilities like those in other countries. Its rise was partly a response to the creation of the European Central Bank.

The European Central Bank (ECB) was founded in 1998. It works in coordination with the member countries' national banks that are part of the ECB issuing the European Union's official currency–the Euro. The national banks are responsible for managing their own economies, but the ECB has sole responsibility for currency management. This awkward arrangement has led to the current Euro crisis. Countries, while not allowed to create Euros per se, are able to issue national debt, which commercial banks purchase by creating Euros. Eventually the European banks wound up holding large amounts of soon to be worthless sovereign debts of Greece, Ireland, Spain, Italy and others. This set off a major banking collapse, which has threatened the solvency of every EU member, even Germany, which is currently facing ratings downgrades on its debt.

Central Banking in the United States

In 1781, Robert Morris, the "Financier of the Revolution", became Superintendent of Finance. Three days later he started the Bank of North America. While privately held, it became the de facto central bank. Large amounts of gold and silver were loaned by France and the Netherlands and served as the bank's startup capital. Its purpose was to finance the Revolutionary War. At times Morris took out personal loans from friends and pledged his own credit by issuing notes to pay the soldiers (who were erratically paid at best). There were many disputes about favoritism, foreign influence and excessive credit creation. In 1791, the Bank of North America handed off the baton of U.S. central bank to the First Bank of the United States.

The First Bank of the United States is a national historic landmark sitting in Philadelphia, Pennsylvania. The United States Congress chartered the bank in February of 1791. Its 20-year charter was created specifically to process financial transactions that the newly fashioned federal government might require. Previously, the thirteen states had been responsible for their own banks and financial institutions.

Alexander Hamilton had pushed for a central bank during the first session of Congress. As the first Secretary of the Treasury, his proposal was lauded by some and viewed suspiciously by others. Many of the Founding Fathers, such as Jefferson and Madison, viewed central banking as a tool of oppression; and for good reason. England had attempted place the colonies under the Bank of England's direct control. Many saw this act as the final straw that led to the American Revolutionary War.

Hamilton proposed funding the First Bank of the United States buy selling $10 million in stock. The United States government was to buy $2 million in shares off the top. The government didn't have it, so Hamilton suggested the bank loan the money to the government for the purchase. The government would pay it back in ten annual installments.

The $8 million in remaining stock would be sold to the public, both foreign and domestic. Non-government entities were required to pay twenty-five percent of the price in silver or gold. This would provide the Bank with $500,000 in real capital.

While Hamilton used the Bank of England as a model for the First Bank of the United States, the primary role he envisioned for it was to be the handling of personal and commercial interests. He felt it was vital for the bank that it be prohibited from purchasing government debt. This was to avoid the well-known abuses of the Bank of England. As a further safeguard, the bank could not issue currency or incur debt above its assets. History shows that Hamilton was prescient on this point.

There were other major differences from the Bank of England as well. Hamilton required the bank be privately held and have a charter that would run for twenty years. During this time, there would be no other federal bank, although the states could establish their own intrastate banks. At the end of the charter, Congress would have the power to either renew the Bank's charter or deny it.

New England merchants and government leaders gave a great deal of support to the central banking scheme, while the southern state representatives were more cautious. As the main trade of the southern states was agriculture, they did not need a central banking system as urgently. Most southerners believed strongly in state's rights and felt that central banking gave too much power to the federal government, enabling it to lord over the individual states.

With the establishment of the First Bank of the United States, Secretary of the Treasury, Alexander Hamilton had many goals. His primary purpose was to create a federal mint and implement an excise tax on alcohol to fund government operations. Hamilton wanted the United States to have financial order that would promote confidence and encourage investment from around the world. Hamilton also saw the need to establish both foreign and domestic credit for the United States. Plus, a mechanism was needed to pay off the continental government's and the state's debts from the Revolutionary War. Finally, Alexander Hamilton wanted to determine what to do about the currency that was in place up until and through the Revolutionary War.

As expected, the Southern Congressional delegations opposed the idea of the central banking system and the establishment of a government mint. Secretary of State Thomas Jefferson and Representative James Madison were vocal in their disapproval, stating that a central bank would be dangerous to the money system. Jefferson and Madison both believed strongly,

45

as did most southerners, that the central banking system would only benefit the northern businesses. Above all else, they argued that the bank would be in direct violation of the Constitution.

The largest concern to the American public was the fear that a monopoly might occur in which interest rates would be raised so high that businesses would be harmed. The bill was passed in three parts. The first part, which established a mint, was quickly passed. The second and third parts of the bill concerned the bank and the tax designed to pay for it.

Because of Madison and Jefferson's objections that the bill violated Constitution's grant of authorized government powers, much debate ensued. However, there really wasn't much choice. As much as the opposition feared the creation of a central bank, they never proposed a workable alternative. They had no plan for dealing with war debt and paying the loyal soldiers who had won the country's independence from England. The final decision eventually found its way to President George Washington. One of the first times that "the buck really did stop here." Washington had a number of reservations, mostly due to his role in setting precedents that would be followed by future presidents. Before signing the bill into law, he solicited and received the opinions of his entire cabinet. Washington then granted Hamilton a chance to rebut. He finally signed the bank bill into law on the 25th of April 1791.

All of which proves that in political debate, principled opposition alone is not always enough. Rather an alternate solution must be debated.

A year later, Congress passed the Coinage Act. Also, known as the Mint Act, it created the United States Mint and set forth the regulation of coinage. The Coinage Act also established the United States' official monetary unit as the dollar, and put the currency on the decimal system, a major improvement from the haphazard denominations of the British system.

Many adjustments have been made to the initial Coinage Act since then, but the essential framework has withstood the test of time. The mint was constructed in Philadelphia, then the nation's capital. The U.S. Mint was the first federal building built under the United States Constitution.

The copper cent was legislated in May of 1792, allowing the mint to buy up to one hundred and fifty tons of copper to coin the money. The Act also stipulated that no other copper money would be legal tender as of that time. Several types of coins were authorized for production and each had specific standards.

Cents and half cents were $0.01 with 11 pennyweights of copper, and $0.005 with 5 ½ pennyweights of copper respectively. Gold coins included eagles, which were $10 pieces of currency made of 270-grains standard gold. Half eagles were worth $5 and made up of 135-grains standard gold. Quarter eagles were $2.50 and contained 67 4/8-grains standard gold.

Silver coins included the dollar, which was worth $1 and made up of 416-grains standard silver. Half dollars were $0.50 each and contained 208-grains standard silver. Quarter dollars were valued at $0.25 and only 104-grains standard silver. "Dismes" (current day Dimes) were worth $0.10 and contained 41 3/5-grains of standard silver. Half "dismes" (current day nickels) were $0.05 and 20 4/5-grains of standard silver.

The original draft coinage bill called for each coin to display an image of the president, but the final draft stated that the coin should display any emblem of liberty. Along with the symbol, the year it was minted and the word "Liberty" was required to inscribed on it. On the backside of each coin there was to be a representation of an eagle as well as the words "United States of America". The copper coins were to be inscribed with the specific denomination, to designate whether it was a cent or half cent.

Many quality control and security measures were also put into place. For example, any employee or officer of the mint could be put to death for fraud, embezzlement, debasing or creating currency at a lesser weight than standard.

This bank's 20-year charter expired in 1811. During its operation, the U.S. government experienced a cash shortage and was forced to sell its Bank shares to raise funds. The Bank didn't go down with out a fight. It lost the charter renewal fight in the House and the Senate by just one vote. Like the Bank of North America before, its charter un-renewed, it eventually gave way to the Second Bank of the United States in 1816. As a footnote, in 1811 after its charter expired, Stephen Girard purchased most of its stock and assets. He then reopened a new bank at the same location that became known as Girard's Bank.

With the creation of the Second Bank of the United States, central banking started anew in the United States. The country had little choice. The War of 1812 ran up substantial debts and ironically led one of its most vocal opponents, President James Madison, to conclude that there was no other way for the country to recover. He felt that independent state banks were not up to the task of paying off the debt and financing economic recovery.

The Second Bank of the United States continued to function well into President Andrew Jackson's presidential term. During the first three years of his presidency, Jackson virtually ignored the bank. In 1832, bank president Nicholas Biddle, pushed for an early charter renewal, which was set to expire in 1836. Jackson's hostility to banks of any description could be traced back to the Panic of 1819. The Second Bank of the U.S. needed to raise gold and silver in to pay off the Louisiana Purchase debt. Pulling this much liquidity out of the system in such a short time caused monetary deflation. Jackson, who was very indebted at the time suffered great financial hardship. He blamed his misfortune on the banks, especially the central bank. Thus begun his lifelong antipathy to all banks that didn't have complete gold or silver backing.

Jackson saw an opportunity to destroy his perceived foe. He vetoed the extension bill. A battle ensued that became known as the Bank War. In 1833 Jackson pulled the government's funds from the Bank. Biddle called loans and reduced the money supply in an attempt to force Jackson's hand. A mild recession ensued in 1834, but Jackson wouldn't relent. The Bank lost its charter in 1836 and struggled on as a state bank until its eventual failure in 1841. Biddle was later tried for fraud and eventually acquitted.

This ended the country's first three experiments with central banking. The U.S. entered a period known as the Free Banking Era, during which there was very little federal bank regulation. Many banks were started and failed.

In an effort to finance the Civil War, a national banking system was created. The idea was to organize the country's financial system, and to replace the diverse regional currencies with a one single national currency. However, without a true central bank, there was no lender of last resort and so banking was still a very risky business.

The Panic of 1907

The Panic of 1907, also known as the 1907 Bankers' Panic is important because it became the rationale for creation of the Federal Reserve. It started when the New York Stock Exchange fell nearly 50 percent from its prior year's high. The country was in the midst of an economic recession and there were numerous runs on banks and trust companies. This was due in part to a lack of liquidity. Major bankers such as JP Morgan refused to extend credit to banks experiencing runs, who he felt were not solvent. The panic began with an effort to corner the market on the United Copper Company's stock. It was underwritten by the Knickerbocker Trust Company of NY, New York's third largest trust. Knickerbocker collapsed, which resulted in a loss of confidence in banks right across the country. However,

JP Morgan intervened, becoming the lender of last resort. Additionally, he helped end the stock market panic by organizing vast buying efforts to restore confidence. The U.S. banking industry's near death experience led to the establishment of a commission by Senator Nelson W. Aldrich (son-in-law of John D. Rockefeller).

The Creature from Jekyll Island

JP Morgan, the Rockefellers and other New York financiers were anxious to avert another bank panic and to prevent bank runs in the future. In 1910 a meeting took place at Jekyll Island, Georgia. Six bankers and economic policy makers who composed the financial elite were present. All participants pledged to absolute secrecy, travelling to the site under assumed names. Their purpose was to devise a central bank. The House of Morgan, the Rockefellers and the Rothschilds, representing approximately 1/6 of the world's wealth were present. Together they came up with and refined the "Aldrich Plan."

The plan provided for a National Reserve Association with 15 regional branches. It would be empowered to make emergency loans to member banks, print money and act as the fiscal agent for the U.S. government. It would be owned by Private banks through a share subscription and ownership formula. There would be no government control of the Reserve, a fact which met with great opposition from rural and western lawmakers, fearful that it would favor the New York "Money Trust" at the exclusion of the common man. The law was debated and modified throughout 1912 and 1913. The final plan eventually provided for a system of public and private entities. It established 12 regional reserve banks, each with their own board of directors and districts. A seven member Federal Reserve Board would head the system. The President would appoint the members, with confirmation by the Senate. From this act was born the infamous Federal Reserve Note.

The bill was pushed through Congress on December 22, 1913 and December 23, 1913. Many lawmakers who opposed the bill had already taken their leave for the Christmas recess. President Woodrow Wilson promptly signed the bill and the United States finally had a central bank. Later Wilson came to lament his decision, stating, "A great industrial nation is controlled by its system of credit. Our system of credit is privately concentrated. The growth of the nation, therefore, and all our activities are in the hands of a few men who, even if their action be honest and intended for the public interest, are necessarily concentrated upon the great undertakings in which their own money is involved and who necessarily, by very reason of their own limitations, chill and check and destroy genuine economic freedom. This is the greatest question of all, and to this statesmen must address themselves with an earnest determination to serve the long future and the true liberties of men."

Here are some interesting and instructive quotes about central banking which provide a necessary perspective on this human endeavor.

"The few who understand the system, will either be so interested from its profits or so dependent on its favors, that there will be no opposition from that class." — Rothschild Brothers of London, 1863

"Give me control of a nation's money and I care not who makes its laws." — Mayer Amschel Bauer Rothschild

Senators & Congressmen:

"Most Americans have no real understanding of the operation of the international money lenders. The accounts of the Federal Reserve System have never been audited. It operates outside the control of Congress and manipulates the credit of the United States"
— Sen. Barry Goldwater (Rep. AZ)

"This [Federal Reserve Act] establishes the most gigantic trust on earth. When the President [Wilson} signs this bill, the invisible government of the monetary power will be legalized....the worst legislative crime of the ages is perpetrated by this banking and currency bill."
— Charles A. Lindbergh, Sr., 1913

"From now on, depressions will be scientifically created."
— Congressman Charles A. Lindbergh Sr., 1913

"The financial system has been turned over to the Federal Reserve Board. That Board administers the finance system by authority of a purely profiteering group. The system is Private, conducted for the sole purpose of obtaining the greatest possible profits from the use of other people's money"
— Charles A. Lindbergh Sr., 1923

"The Federal Reserve bank buys government bonds without one penny..."
— Congressman Wright Patman, Congressional Record, Sept 30, 1941

"We have, in this country, one of the most corrupt institutions the world has ever known. I refer to the Federal Reserve Board. This evil institution has impoverished the people of the United States and has practically bankrupted our government. It has done this through the corrupt practices of the moneyed vultures who control it".
— Congressman Louis T. McFadden in 1932 (Rep. Pa)

"The Federal Reserve banks are one of the most corrupt institutions the world has ever seen. There is not a man within the sound of my voice who does not know that this nation is run by the International bankers
— Congressman Louis T. McFadden (Rep. Pa)

"Some people think the Federal Reserve Banks are the United States government's institutions. They are not government institutions. They are private credit monopolies which prey upon the people of the United States for the benefit of themselves and their foreign swindlers"
– Congressional Record 12595-12603
— Louis T. McFadden, Chairman of the Committee on Banking and Currency (12 years) June 10, 1932

Fractional Reserve Banking

Investopedia defines Fractional Reserve Banking as, "A banking system in which only a fraction of bank deposits are backed by actual cash-on-hand and are available for withdrawal. This is done to expand the economy by freeing up capital that can be loaned out to other parties. All countries operate under this type of system."

Fractional reserve banking is the key enabler that allows private banks to create money out of thin air. For every dollar deposited in a bank, it is required to keep a certain percentage in reserve. These funds cannot be loaned out to borrowers. They are kept at the ready to satisfy their depositor's possible desire to withdraw their funds. The reserve is kept as cash on hand. Also known as a cash reserve ratio, it is the percentage of deposits that a central bank requires banks to keep on hand. Over the years, this number has been declining. The Bank for International Settlements, a sort of super central bank has set requirements for bank capitalization that are beginning to take hold. Based on past performance, we'll have to see whether the rules are allowed to take effect, and how they will affect the dire situation the world's banks currently find themselves in.

The flaws of this system became very apparent during the Great Depression. Once confidence was lost in the banking system, depositors lined up around the block demanding return of their funds. Since the banks had at most just 10 percent of their deposits on hand, the result was massive bank closures. The Federal Reserve was supposed to be at the ready as the "lender of last resort" to stop this from happening. But for reasons already discussed, they failed in this regard.

Today, at present, they have backstopped virtually every bank in the Country, and perhaps the world, to insure that no depositor loses any funds. While certain losses have occurred on larger accounts, they have mostly been successful in stabilizing the system. The question is: when there's a large loss of confidence in one or more Too Big to Fail banks, what will they do? Will they print currency units and pay everyone off and perhaps leave the dollar decimated, or will they only honor a percentage of the bank's obligations? Based on recent behavior and the Treasury and Fed's willingness to underwrite virtually any loss the banks have realized, such as Citibank and Bank of America, the answer is your deposits are currently as safe as the dollar. If past is prologue, they will continue to be.

How It Works

It is quite difficult to calculate the actual reserve requirement. While U.S. banks are required to keep 10 percent of their deposits for transaction accounts (checking) on hand, there is no reserve requirement for time deposits, i.e. certificates of deposit. The large banks' borrowings from the Federal Reserve have escalated to a point that it is quite possible that much of their so-called reserve is made up of funds borrowed directly from the Fed.

Banks are in the business of loaning money to earn income. Their profit is the differential between the rate which they can realize on loans minus the cost that they pay for funds (interest on your bank account). Obviously, modern banking has become much more complex, with derivatives, securities underwritings and many other fee generating opportunities that the banking industry has exploited. But the way that banks print money out of thin air has remained a mystery to most people in the country, if not the world. It is this ability to print money that makes a banking license or franchise so potentially profitable and dangerous.

They typically lend out most of the deposited funds in an effort to earn money by way of interest payments. Money loaned is deposited into the lending bank or to other banks. What happens is that the money is effectively borrowed into existence, as the bank keeps the mon???????? and thereby increases the supply of money in a country. Banks also spend depositor's money on securities as a way to earn money and expand the money supply.

Many countries have a money supply that is much broader than the base amount of money that has been created by the central bank. Financial regulators limit the money multiplier by use of the reserve requirement, effectively establishing the percentage of money the bank is not allowed to loan out or spend on securities. By requiring commercial banks to keep a portion of deposited money in reserve, there will theoretically be enough money to meet the regular demand for withdrawals of their customers. Occasionally there can be problems if a large number of depositors wish to withdraw their money at the same time. Bank runs or systemic crises can occur in this instance, causing widespread financial catastrophes. This is one reason the central banks work to regulate the commercial banks and act as a lender of last resort. It is their efforts which keep the system afloat while protecting the commercial bank's customer deposits.

Do Not Try This At Home

If you're anyone other than a member bank of the Federal Reserve, you'll will likely be prosecuted and sent to jail for doing what they do. Fractional Reserve Banking is one huge Ponzi scheme that allows an increase in the supply of currency available to make loans to purchase investment capital, without increasing the national quantity of investment capital or real savings.

If the reserve requirement is 10%, for example, a bank that receives a $100 deposit may lend out $90 of that deposit. If the borrower then writes a check to someone who deposits the $90, the bank receiving that deposit can lend out $81. As the process continues, the banking system can expand the initial deposit of $100 into a maximum of $1,000 of money ($100 + $90 + 81 + $72.90 + ... = $1,000).

The Current Monetary Crisis

In 2008, the world found itself in yet another monetary crisis. Where previous monetary collapses were often isolated to individual countries or regions, this one has been felt in every corner of an increasingly shrinking globe. Although many reasons exist for the malaise, the major one can be traced right back to the doorstep of the world's central banks and the Federal Reserve.

These institutions which were ostensibly created to assure economic and financial stability have become victims of their own success. As long as they kept money creation at or about the level of increased productivity, plus two percent, currency values would stay the same and the world's population would be none the wiser about the gradual debasement taking place.

Once the dollar became the world's de facto reserve currency, and President Nixon severed the last remaining link to the gold standard in 1971, it was just a matter of time until the world would be confronted by the current crisis. The average fiat money system lasts about 40 years. By this standard, the fiat dollar would appear to be on its last legs.

The Federal Reserve continues to produce an endless flood of digital dollars. The money supply has more than doubled over the past three years. As the largest holder of U.S. government debt, the Federal Reserve far outstrips the prior record holders, China and Japan.

With all these factors going against it, how much longer can the dollar hold out? One would expect an eventual loss of faith in the dollar as a store of value. Once this occurs, the race will be on to convert worthless dollars into hard goods. This phase won't last for long, the result will be a complete worldwide economic meltdown. It would be the end of fiat money as we know it. As a result the globe's inhabitants would be distrustful of paper money for several generations.

The main question on everyone's mind is when will this cataclysmic event take place? And the answer, as always remains murky. There is no effective means to predict when a certain inevitable event will take place.

Every human being on planet earth knows their time is limited, but they have no idea when their last day will be. Someone who's 90 years old can be pretty certain that their day will come before a 16 year old's.

However, there are key indicators that could provide a small glimpse of warning. Long-term dips in the USD index are one possibility. However, this has become less meaningful as the Euro and other world's currencies either get sick, or are devalued to maintain a competitive trade advantage.

Another important sign is large, almost panicked, increases in precious metals prices. We have periodically seen such days, especially during the summer of 2011, when gold and silver went up as much as 4 percent in a single day. While the metals have been in a super-bull market for the past decade, they have suffered some substantial retrenchments in the past year. The $2000 gold price and $50 silver price are key measures. When these levels are exceeded, this will be a sure sign that the paper-money scam is nearing an end.

Perhaps the best sign of impending currency doom is imposition of capital controls. Virtually every country facing a currency collapse resorts to this ineffective act of desperation, shortly before the event becomes a reality. At the same time, the very politicians imposing the controls will be shipping their assets out of the country en masse. In actuality, no further signs are necessary. Rather, the process has begun and momentum is building behind it.

Unless our country and the world drastically change their evil ways of consuming more than they produce, cut their budgets and embrace sound money, then history will repeat itself. It does so with alarming regularity and the dollar and its fiat compatriots cannot avoid their fate.

The U.S., while not imposing explicit capital controls, appears headed in that direction. For nearly two decades, Americans have been required to declare to authorities their possession of over $10,000 in currency when leaving the country. Congress has adopted onerous reporting requirements for foreign banks accepting deposits from American clients. This has resulted in most of the world's banks and brokerage houses refusing to accept American clients. Such measures have the effect of currency controls without the stigma associated with outright bans. Look for the noose to continue to tighten, and when all circulation has been cut-off, you will know that end game is here.

Fiat Currency Always Dies

Fiat Currency: Using the Past to See into the Future

Reprinted with Permission by Agora Financial:
dailyreckoning.com/fiat-currency/

Fiat Money -Toilet Paper Money

The history of fiat money, to put it kindly, has been one of failure. In fact, EVERY fiat currency since the Romans first began the practice in the first century has ended in devaluation and eventual collapse, of not only the currency, but of the economy that housed the fiat currency as well.

Why would it be different here in the U.S.? Well, in actuality, it hasn't been. In fact, in our short history, we've already had several failed attempts at using paper currency, and it is my opinion that today's dollars are no different than the continentals issued during the Revolutionary War. But I will get into that in a moment. In the meantime, I will show you that fiat currencies have not been successful, and the only aspect of fiat currencies that have stood the test of time is the inability of political systems to prevent the devaluation and debasement of this toilet paper money by letting the printing presses run wild.

Fiat Money -Rome – The Denarius

Although Rome didn't actually have paper money, it provided one of the first examples of true debasement of a currency. The denarius, Rome's coinage of the time, was, essentially, pure silver at the beginning of the first century A.D. By A.D. 54, Emperor Nero had entered the scene, and the denarius was approximately 94% silver. By around A.D.100, the denarius' silver content was down to 85%.

Emperors that succeeded Nero liked the idea of devaluing their currency in order to pay the bills and increase their own wealth. By 218, the denarius was down to 43% silver, and in 244, Emperor Philip the Arab had the silver content dropped to 0.05%. Around the time of Rome's collapse, the denarius contained – only 0.02% silver and virtually nobody accepted it as a medium of exchange or a store of value.

Fiat Money – China – Flying Money

When the Chinese first started using paper money, they called it "flying money," because it could just fly from your hands. The reason for the issuance of paper money is simple. There was a copper shortage, so banks had switched to the use of iron coinage. These iron coins became over issued and fell in value.

In the 11th century, a bank in the Szechuan province of China issued paper money in exchange for the iron coins. Initially, this was fine, because the paper money was exchangeable for gold, silver, or silk. Eventually, inflation began to take hold, as China was funding an ongoing war with the Mongols, which it eventually lost.

Genghis Khan won this war, but the Mongols didn't assume immediate control over China as they pushed westward to conquer more lands. Genghis Khan's grandson Kublai Khan united China and assumed the emperorship. After running into some setbacks with paper currency, Kublai eventually had some success with fiat money. In fact, Marco Polo said of Kublai Khan and the use of paper currency:

"You might say that [Kublai] has the secret of alchemy in perfection... the Khan causes every year to be made such a vast quantity of this money, which costs him nothing, that it must equal in amount all the treasure of the world."

Even Helicopter Ben would be impressed. Marco Polo went on to say:

"This was the most brilliant period in the history of China. Kublai Khan, after subduing and uniting the whole country and adding Burma, Cochin China, and Tonkin to the empire, entered upon a series of internal improvements and civil reforms, which raised the country he had conquered to the highest rank of civilization, power, and progress."

Wait a second, I thought we were bashing fiat currencies here ... Can anyone say crackup boom? Since Marco Polo experienced this firsthand, and has been very helpful to us thus far, I think I will allow him to finish his analysis of China's paper money experiment.

"Population and trade had greatly increased, but the emissions of paper notes were suffered to largely outrun both...All the beneficial effects of a currency that is allowed to expand with a growth of population and trade were now turned into those evil effects that flow from a currency emitted in excess of such growth. These effects were not slow to develop themselves...

The best families in the empire were ruined, a new set of men came into the control of public affairs, and the country became the scene of internecine warfare and confusion."

I wonder if Keynes read Marco Polo's experiences with Chinese fiat currencies when he said that the U.S. government should just bury bottles full of money in old mine shafts to spur economic growth.

***Fiat Money** -France – Livres, Assignats, and Francs*

The French have been particularly unsuccessful in their attempts with fiat money.

John Law was the first man to introduce paper money to France. The notion of paper money was greatly helped along by the passing of Louis XIV and the 3 billion livres of debt that he left.

When Louis XV was old enough to make his own mistakes, he required that all taxes be paid in paper money. The currency was backed by coinage… until people actually wanted coins.

The theme of the day … the new paper currency rapidly became oversupplied until nobody wished to own the worthless junk anymore and demanded coinage for their currency.

Oops. It looks like Law didn't think that anyone would actually want coins ever again. After making it illegal to export any gold or silver, and the failed attempts by the locals to exchange their paper currency for something of actual value, the currency collapsed.

John Law became the most hated man in France and was forced to flee to Italy.

In the latter part of the 18th century, the French government again tried to give paper money another go. This time, the pieces of garbage they issued were called assignats. By 1795, inflation of assignats was running at approximately 13,000%. Oops. Then Napoleon stepped on the scene and brought with him the gold franc. One of the good things that Napoleon realized is that gold is the way of a stable currency, and that's what pretty much ensued during his reign.

After Waterloo had come and gone, the French gave it another go in the 1930s, this time with the paper franc. It took only 12 years for them to inflate their currency until it lost 99% of its value. History has proven a couple things about the French:

1) They are quick to surrender and

2) They are very talented at making worthless currency.

Weimar Germany – Mark

Post-World War I Weimar Germany was one of the greatest periods of hyperinflation that ever existed. The Treaty of Versailles was essentially a financial punishment placed on Germany to make reparations.

The sums of money to be paid by Germany were enormous, and the only way it could make repayment was by running the printing press. (Huge unpayable debt – that sounds familiar. I wonder what the solution in the U.S. will be.)

Inflation got so bad in this period that German citizens were literally using stacks of marks to heat their furnaces. Here is a brief timeline of the marks per one U.S. dollar exchange rate:

April 1919: 12 marks
November 1921: 263 marks
January 1923: 17,000 marks
August 1923: 4.621 million marks
October 1923: 25.26 billion marks
December 1923: 4.2 trillion marks.

***Fiat Money** -More Recent Times*

In recent times, fiat failures have become more common occurrences. For the sake of time, I won't go into extensive details of all these examples of paper money failures, because there are SO many. But here you have it:

In 1932, Argentina had the eighth largest economy in the world before its currency collapsed. In 1992, Finland, Italy, and Norway had currency shocks that spread through Europe.

In 1994, Mexico went through the infamous "Tequila Hangover," which sent the peso tumbling and spread economic hardships throughout Latin America.

In 1997, the Thai baht fell through the floor and the effects spread to Malaysia, the Philippines, Indonesia, Hong Kong, and South Korea.

The Russian ruble was not the currency you wanted your investments denominated in 1998, after its devaluation brought on economic recession. In the early 21st century, we have seen the Turkish lira experience strokes of hyperinflation similar to that of the mark of Weimar Germany.

In present times, we have Zimbabwe, which was once considered the breadbasket of Africa and was one of the wealthiest countries on the continent. Now Mugabe's attempts at price controls, combined with hyperinflation, have the nation unable to supply the most basic essentials such as bread and clean water.

***Fiat Money** -Lessons to Be Learned*

Here in the U.S., I should say the lessons were not learned. There are many consistencies from the above-mentioned stories that led up to the eventual collapse of the currencies.

The scary thing is that the U.S. has some of these above-mentioned characteristics, the ones that lead to toilet paper money becoming just that. More on that in just a second. I would first like to give a brief look at the U.S. attempts with paper money in our short history.

The first attempt with paper money came in 1690 with the issuance of Colonial notes. The first Colonial notes were issued in Massachusetts and were redeemable for gold, silver, corn, cattle and other commodities.

The other Colonies quickly jumped on the toilet paper money bandwagon and began issuing their own paper currencies. Like a broken record, the money quickly became over issued. The lessons of John Law and others were definitely not learned. It is not good enough just to say that a currency is backed by commodities. It actually HAS to be backed by commodities. Essentially, it was still a fiat money, and in a short period of time, Colonials became as good as toilet paper.

The next experiment came during the Revolutionary War. Big surprise – the issuance of paper money was used to finance the war efforts. This time, the currency was called a continental.

The crash of the continental was spectacular, and the phrase "not worth a continental" was coined. This brought on a large distrust for paper currency, and until 1913, toilet paper money in the U.S. wasn't used. Enter the infamous Federal Reserve and its monopoly on money and interest rates. Now we have the greenback.

Although the money was "officially" backed by a gold standard until 1971, it wasn't a true gold standard. When the government found it inconvenient to have a gold standard, it just made it illegal for U.S. citizens to hold gold or exchange dollars for gold.

As reported on Strike-the-root.com:

"Under the infallible leadership of President Franklin Roosevelt, it was made illegal to own gold. On March 11, 1933, he issued an order forbidding banks to make gold payments. On April 5, Roosevelt ordered all citizens to surrender their gold – no person could hold more than $100 in gold coins, except for collector's coins. He also made it unlawful to export gold for payment abroad, unless done through the Treasury. The penalty for defying Roosevelt was 10 years in prison and a $250,000 fine."

But the official demise of the dollar was locked into place in 1971 when "Tricky Dick" Nixon completely severed all ties between the dollar and the gold standard. During the decade that followed, the U.S. experienced some of the worst inflation in its history, only matched by today's U.S. monetary and fiscal irresponsibility.

The U.S. of A. has all the characteristics set in place that have led to the collapse of every other fiat currency money in history.

We are currently at war, and the financing of this war is extremely inflationary. In fact, if you look back at our history, since 1914, the U.S has engaged in 16 military conflicts. We have been involved in some form of violent international accord in 44 of the past 93 years. The overwhelming majority of military conflicts result in monetary inflation.

The U.S. has a debt similar to that of Weimar Germany. All though the reasons for the debt are completely different, it appears that this Mount Everest of IOUs is going to be impossible to pay back. I guess the U.S. could just print 10 trillion dollar bills and hand them out, but the implications of such actions are obvious.

We are currently increasing the supply of dollars at a rate of 13% per annum. This over issuance of a currency has been the leading indicator of a currency on the brink.

So what's in the future for the dollar?

Some, myself included, might say that the dollar has already failed. It has lost over 92% of its value since its initial issuance in 1913. After the revaluation in 1934, the dollar dropped another 41%. In my opinion, it already is toilet paper money, but for the above-mentioned characteristics, which are alarmingly similar to the circumstances that led up to the eventual collapse of the dollar's toilet paper predecessors, I believe that we have seen only the tip of the iceberg of the dollar's inevitable path toward becoming toilet paper money.

How Much Gold is Really in Fort Knox

The U.S. Treasury/Federal Reserve claim that the U.S. has 8,133.5 tons in storage at several vaults across the Country, including Fort Knox, West Point and perhaps the New York Federal Reserve Building on Liberty Street in Lower Manhattan. But there hasn't been an audit, where auditors actually go to the vaults and count the bars and record their serial numbers since the 1954. The last "audit" of gold reserves supposedly took place in 2005. But according to KPMG LLP, they only audited the mint's fiscal year 2005 financial statements. They never saw any physical gold or even went to Fort Knox.

The Dollar is a Debt Based Currency

The dollar bill isn't a bill; it's a note, evidence of indebtedness. This is an important distinction. A bill is an asset; a note's a liability. Federal Reserve notes are liabilities of the Federal Reserve. But how do these notes come into being. One of several ways. First, the Federal Government through the Treasury creates a bond. They will sell it to individuals, who will take their savings and purchase the debt or to the Federal Reserve. When the Fed purchases Treasury debt (bonds, notes, etc.) they pay with money created out of thin air. For example; if the Fed purchases a $1 million bond, it simply writes a check to the Treasury. Where does the money come from, why the Fed just "prints" it up. They do an electronic transfer from their account into the Treasury's. Wish you could do the same? Think how great life would be, want that Bentley, just write a check and not worry where the money comes from. Great isn't it? It's good to be the Fed, even better than being the King.

Who Owns the Fed?

As one commentator put it, the Federal Reserve is about as federal as Federal Express and isn't really a reserve either. There have been many claims that the Fed is actually owned by foreign banking interests, most notably the Rothschilds. Dr. Edward Flaherty concluded that the major money center banks appear on their face to be independent of foreign control. They are the effective owners of the Fed, while the President appoints the governors, with the advice and consent of the senate.

Now of course everyone is convinced, including the author, that the Congress is owned by the financial industry. They raise much of their campaign funds there and in exchange they grant valuable favors to the industry. Look at the way TARP (Troubled Assets Relief Program) was pushed through both Houses, with minimal debate. In addition, it was recently disclosed that at the height of the financial crisis, the Fed "loaned" banks across the globe over $16 trillion. We have no idea why the money was loaned, if it has been paid back and what the terms of the "loans" were.

So is ownership an important matter? Because of the nation's rapid debt escalation, the Fed is collecting more and more interest, the Treasury is simply giving bonds to the Fed and receiving the cash to finance the federal government. Fed profits have been escalating as well. Historically, the majority of the Fed's profits were paid back to the Treasury, the net effect being that the interest paid on government debt, came back to the treasury, in the process reducing the deficit by the amount received. But all that changed in 2010. The Fed now keeps those funds to do with as it chooses, and so far they haven't told us what their purpose is. In 2011 they kept $77 billion. No doubt in 2012 the amount will be even larger. But that "profit" came from the Treasury's interest payments to the Fed. The U.S. Government budget deficit has been effectively increased by that amount. How this is beneficial to our national finances is a mystery.

Where Are We Now?

If one thing is clear from the previous exposition on money and precious metals, every fiat (unbacked) currency eventually realizes its intrinsic value, zero. It becomes worth less than the paper it's printed on. As Ludwig von Mises is quoted as saying, "Government is the only entity in the world that can take a perfectly valuable commodity like paper and make it worthless by applying ink."

Paper currency isn't as popular a medium of exchange as it once was. The latest estimate of total currency (coins and notes) in circulation is around $829 billion. However the amount of electronic currency in circulation is many times greater. M0 (monetary base) is $2.4 trillion. M1 (U.S. money stock, currency in circulation plus demand accounts) is $2.269 trillion. M2 (M1 plus savings accounts) is close to $10 trillion. The Fed stopped posting the statistics on M3, which is M2 plus all institutional money market funds, short-term repo agreements and a lot of other high finance vehicles. In the name of saving money, perhaps a few million per year, the Fed stopped publishing this number 2006. A specious argument at best. While the total amount out there is important, in and of itself it means nothing. Rather, what is more important is the trend of the supply, and in this case it is nothing short of frightening. We will take the M0 chart, which is the so-called monetary base, which is money that the banks have on deposit with the Fed as reserves. All other money in the system is leveraged off of the base. From the base you can almost leverage to infinity.

A look at the chart below tells the story of the dollar's debasement far better than any words possibly could.

U.S. Dollar Purchasing Power:
Gold Standard vs. Fiat Currency

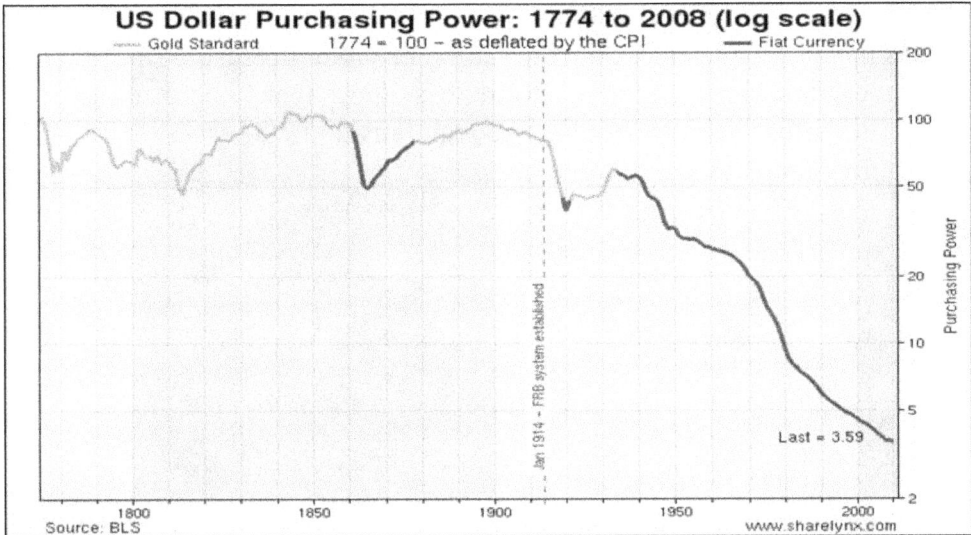

U.S. Dollar Purchasing Power 1914 Onwards Including
ShadowStats Estimate

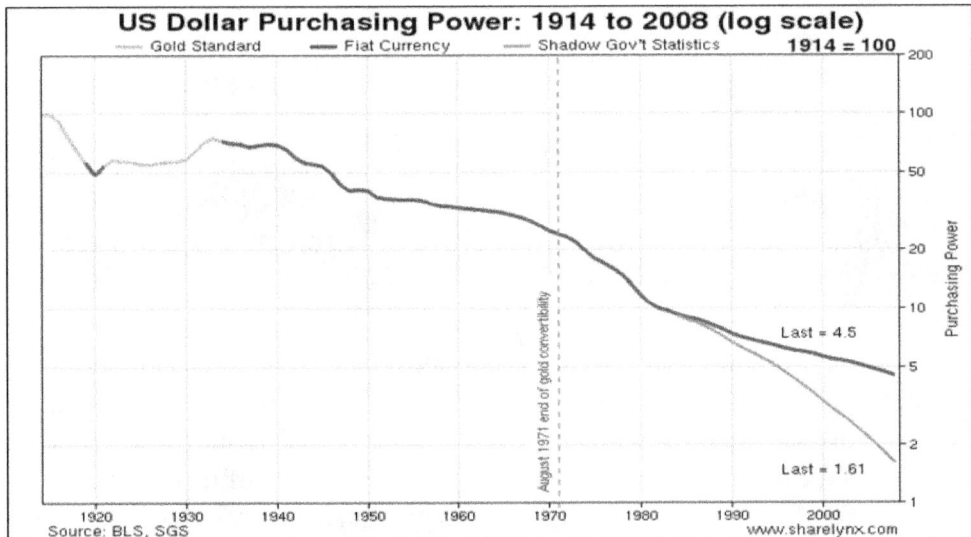

The monetary base or M0 is a little published statistic that tells us a lot about our current economic climate and the eventual death of the modern dollar. The base is the amount of cash and reserves that is deposited by commercial banks with the Federal Reserve. Based on these reserves, this will determine how much credit the banks are allowed to extend. Notice that in 1985 the base was around 200 billion dollars. Fast-forward to 2012 and the base is now a staggering $2.6 trillion, or a ten-fold increase. Prior to 2007, it was very unusual for the base to increase more than 5 percent per year. Since 2007 it has been increasing exponentially.

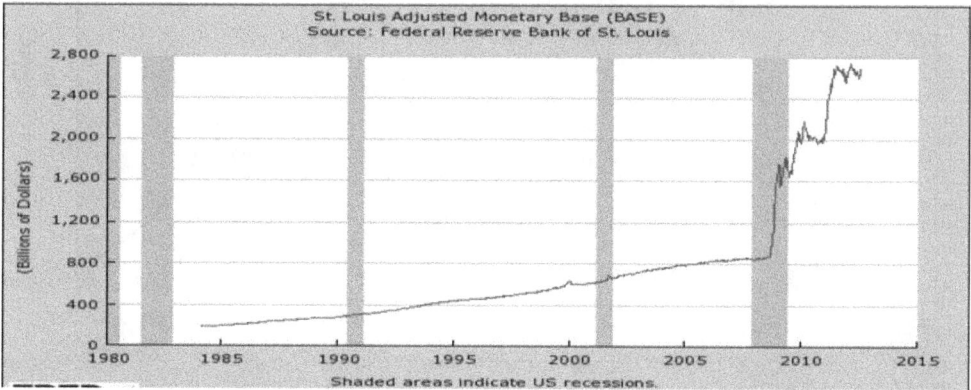

The total money stock has seen a similar increase and its chart is almost as scary as MO.

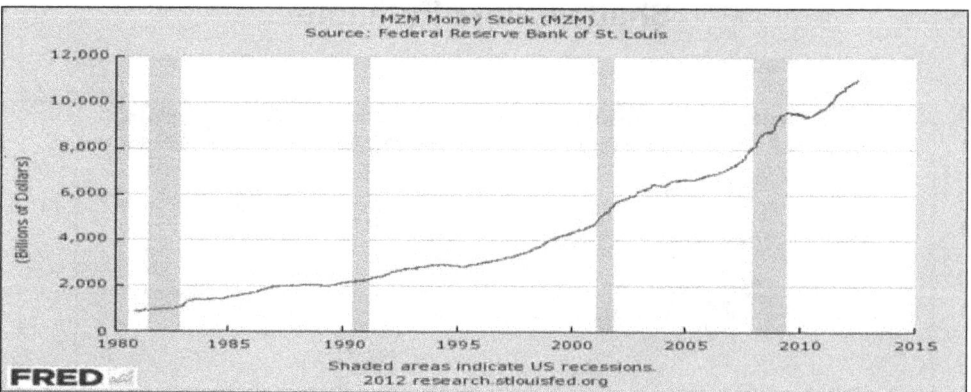

Core inflation, the government assures us has been virtually non-existent. Of course food and energy costs have been excluded from this equation. As long as you don't drive a car and produce all your food yourself, then you have been exempt from inflation too. For those of us who buy food in a supermarket and fill our vehicles with gasoline, several times per week, we have been suffering from inflation. In addition, we have seen health insurance, property taxes, electricity, education and many other costs increase at double-digit rates. Because the government overweighs the cost of home ownership in their formula, there have been times when prices have actually appeared to fall, when in fact they have been rising.

Annual Consumer Inflation - Official vs SGS (1980-Based) Alternate
Year to Year Change. Through June 2012. (BLS, SGS)

— SGS Alternate CPI, 1980-Based   — CPI-U

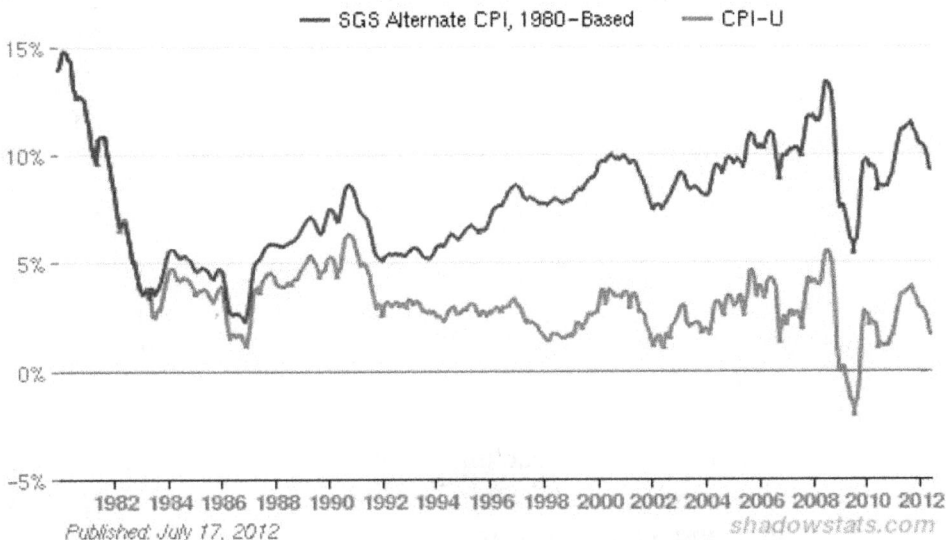

Published: July 17, 2012   shadowstats.com

Annual Consumer Inflation - Official vs SGS (1990-Based) Alternate
CPI-U Year to Year Change. Not Seasonally Adjusted. to June 2012 (BLS, SGS)

— Official CPI-U   Experimental C-CPI   — SGS Alternate 1990-Based

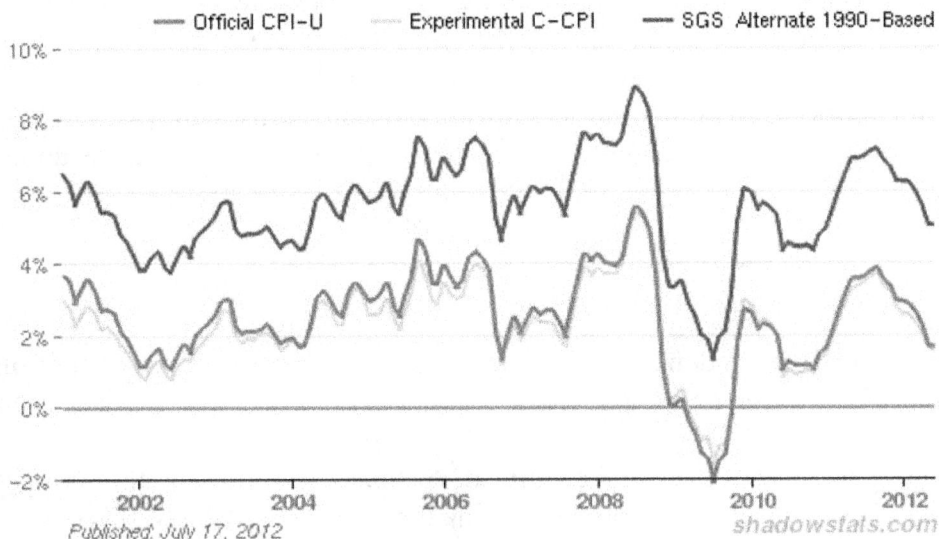

Published: July 17, 2012   shadowstats.com

With Quantitative Easing (QE), 1, 2, Lite, 3... becoming the rule, it is quite obvious that high rates of inflation, if not hyperinflation, will be with us for a long time to come. Currencies can continue losing value for many years, before experiencing the ultimate death knell. What commentators refuse to discuss is that the Federal Reserve and the Treasury have no choice but to inflate the currency. The government is spending $3.8 trillion per year. It can only bring in about $2.1 trillion in taxes. Therefore, the money to finance the ever-increasing size of government must come from somewhere. The world is now limiting its purchases of U.S. government debt. While the Euro turmoil has increased the desirability of Treasury Debt in the U.S. as well as Germany and Switzerland, this illusion of the dollar being a safe haven can't last much longer. Where is the money going to come from? Therefore, the United States is in a trap. To bring the budget into balance would require a forty percent cut to the budget. There is no possible way that either party will agree to such a "draconian" cut. They believe that they can just keep "kicking the can down road," and let a future congress deal with this intractable problem.

But the road is rapidly reaching a dead end. Add to this, the country's depleted industrial base, failing educational system, more people receiving benefits than paying taxes, insolvent financial sector and hundreds trillions in bets known as derivatives, and you see that the current system is beyond hope and that no cure is possible. This means that the United States will default on its debt. Either spending is cut and the country collapses triggering a default, but at least the currency stays in tact, or more dollars keep getting created out of thin air, bringing about hyperinflation. The currency becomes worthless and all debt gets paid in full. And even if hyperinflation never kicks in, when the real rate of inflation hits 10 percent per year, the effects upon the average American's standard of living will be devastating.

Things Are Not Getting Better-
They're Getting Worse

The budget deficit and the trade deficit are completely out of control. The U.S. has been running 1.5 trillion dollar deficits for the past 3 years and 2012 to 2020 will be much the same. The world's appetite for U.S. government debt appears to be quite satiated. At the present time, with the prospects and an all out Euro crash appearing more likely by the day, this market has become somewhat of a safe haven for capital escaping Europe's shaky banks. In 2011 the Federal Reserve purchased 61 percent of the nation's new treasury debt. This year might be a bit lower, but once the European situation sorts itself out, investors will no longer be longer to the U.S. for risk-free investing.

The trade deficit is equally alarming. While it is down from its previous high in 2007, it has kicked up a bit and represents the country's excess consumption over what it produces. While countries such as China, India, Saudi Arabia have been content to take U.S. IOU's in the form of currency, the confidence in those IOU's is eroding and one day there won't be an appetite for any more.

Then we examine the true unemployment rate, again compliments of Mr. Williams and Shadowstats.com. We see that the unemployment rate, the way it was once calculated is nearly 23 percent, representing a near depression level. During the great depression, the level hit a high of 25 percent. We can easily envision it going higher this time around, since it appears we haven't yet hit the peak.

Finally, yet another horrid indicator is the number of people currently on food stamps or their electronic equivalent, the EBT card. A staggering 46.5 million people are receiving them as of this date. And the government is advertising for more recipients and is even working with countries like Mexico to increase the number recipient base. Obviously some of the collectivists among us won't be happy until the entire country is swiping their EBT cards at the supermarket cashier.

The Time is Now

The current estimate is that less than five percent of the population, and perhaps as little as two percent of the population, own any precious metals. This means is that virtually all of the country is oblivious to the coming collapse and virtually no one will be spared the devastation. Are they in denial, on drugs or alcohol or just too busy focusing on Charlie Sheen's and Lindsay Lohan's latest drug crazed exploits? That will be for the historians to determine. For now, let's just assume that this is a case of mass denial. If the theory is correct that a massive economic collapse is all but inevitable, and that few people have prepared for it, then a disaster of truly biblical proportions is on the way. If the trucks and the trains ever stop running, supermarkets will run out of food in just days.

If you can see the handwriting on the wall, how can you prepare. First, you must have at least a minimal supply of gold and silver safely stored to help protect you against any such eventuality. The prices of these metals have been increasing dramatically. Since the 2000 gold bottom, gold has gone from $252 to over $1950 (currently around $1600) in the past decade. Silver has increased even more dramatically, from $5 to over $46 (currently around $27) in the similar time period.

The evidence shows that these are heavily manipulated markets. Allegations of massive collusion between the U.S. Government and the large financial institutions, such as Goldman Saks, JP Morgan Chase and HSBC have been brought and appear to be valid. There are claims that this group has used the futures markets in London, New York and Chicago to artificially suppress the metal prices. Some proof has been furnished, but it is an extremely difficult allegation to prove. By its very nature, such a conspiracy would have to be conducted with the utmost secrecy. Any leaks or evidence getting expose would immediately be its downfall and perhaps a major collapse. However, the markets have been behaving in such anomalous fashion, that experienced investors believe that something is clearly up.

For the average American/Investor all this conspiracy talk is completely irrelevant. If your government is actually suppressing the price of gold and silver, this means you are getting a government subsidy every time you make a purchase. If the government wants to make it cheaper and easier for you to acquire metals, then be grateful because in the long run it will be one of the very few favors they have done for you.

The question arises, how much total gold and silver should you own? And how much of each? There is no exact answer to this question as it completely depends upon individual circumstances. The system is so far gone and its demise so certain, that in the long term any purchases will clearly yield tremendous returns (sometimes a tremendous return can be defined as simply not losing your money).

In the short and intermediate term, there have been and there will continue to be corrections and downturns. Silver's near parabolic rise is a case in point. Having quintupled since its October 2009 lows, reaching almost $50 per ounce, silver has pulled back, hitting lows in the $26 range, while currently trading at around $28. Silver, being the more volatile of the two metals, it always has more violent and larger corrections than gold. A rapid fifty percent decline is not at all unusual. It happened in 2009 going from $21 per ounce to less than $9, in just weeks. It happened again in 2011 from $49.50 to $26. In the current market conditions, anything is possible.

The important thing to remember is that no one can predict metals prices day by day, except perhaps JP Morgan and the Fed. Any effort to predict a price at a certain date is destined for failure. It just doesn't work. When gold hit $1950 in the summer of 2011, everyone was bracing for the ultimate break out. They were all wrong, the author included. Always remember that any market, both by accident or design, always frustrates and defeats the majority of participants. This is always true over the short run, and mostly true over the long haul.

Follow the Money

Reprinted with permission by: Eric Sprott & Andrew Morris

You know silver's doing well when the commentators start giving it the 'gold' treatment. Silver's recent rise has been so spectacular that it's caught many investors off guard. It's natural to be skeptical when you don't know the fundamentals driving strong performance, and many pundits and commentators have been quick to downplay it as a result - much like they do towards gold when it enjoys a run. Silver is also an awkward metal for them to categorize. Is it a commodity, a monetary metal, or both? And which side is driving demand? If it's industrial demand, that's okay, because that's bullish. But if it's investment demand for silver as 'money', well then that's sort of bearish, isn't it? The fact remains that most commentators have failed to grasp the monetary shifts that silver is signaling today, and in doing so they've failed to appreciate just how high it could actually go.

The financial media's failure to grasp the benefits of precious metals ownership continues to perplex us, and it's not just the commentators who are prone to perpetual disbelief. The sell side analysts are equally as irresolute. According to Bloomberg, the 'expert' consensus silver price forecast for 2011 is $29.50, representing a 31% discount from the current spot price. This same group of analysts also predicts prices will decline another 25% in 2012 and a further 9% in 2013 to $20 an ounce. When you consider that the silver price has appreciated by over 21% annually over the past 10 years, these forecasts suggest a very dramatic change in the long-term trend. Will this reversal come true? Probably not. These were the same analysts who predicted that spot silver prices would average $18.65 this year - so they've missed the mark by over 100% thus far.

We don't mean to bash the silver analyst community, and there are several whom we highly respect, but it is important for silver investors to appreciate that these price forecasts are being plugged into financial models that dictate equity valuations. These models are used by traders, bankers, analysts, and portfolio managers to derive valuations for silver stocks and create asset allocations for portfolios. To anyone questioning current silver equity valuations, we would ask: what price assumptions are you using? Of course we, as allocators, of capital are thankful for this phenomenon, as it allows us to buy our favorite silver stocks on the cheap, knowing full well that the herd will be following behind in due course as those back-ward-looking forecasts get ratcheted higher.

How can we be so confident that the price of silver will continue on its upward trajectory? Our thesis is premised on the most rudimentary of economic principles – supply and demand.

One of the key indicators that we've been monitoring is the gold/silver ratio. Much has been written about the ratio of late, and we won't go into great detail on the subject, other than to note that the last time money was synonymous with defined amounts of gold and silver, the ratio was set at 16-to-one. In fact, for most of the past millennium, one ounce of gold would have been convertible to somewhere between 10 and 16 ounces of silver - an amount roughly in line with the relative occurrence of each mineral within the earth's crust.

1. For the better part of the past century, due to the world's abandonment of bimetallism and then the gold standard, the gold/silver ratio has fluctuated widely, twice reaching lows near the 15-to-one mark and a high of 100-to-one back in the early 1990's. The most recent high reached in the latter part of 2009 was nearly 80-to-one. Since then the ratio has been tumbling to where it stands now at 35-to-one – which reflects the incredible outperformance of silver over that time period. In our opinion, this ratio will continue to move lower, driven by nothing more than basic supply/demand fundamentals.

The U.S. Mint, which is the world's largest silver and gold coin manufacturer, recently reported that it had sold 13 million ounces of silver coins and 370 thousand ounces of gold coins on a year-to-date basis.

2. This means that the U.S. Mint is now selling roughly equal amounts of silver and gold in dollars so far this year. Furthermore, bullion dealers like Sprott Money and Gold Money have confirmed with us that they are now selling more silver than gold in dollar terms. For additional confirmation of this investment trend, just look at the flows for the two largest gold and silver ETFs. Investors have withdrawn approximately $3 billion from the GLD so far this year while the SLV has seen net inflows of $370 million over the same period. Dollar for dollar, investors are allocating as much if not more money to silver than to gold. And why shouldn't they?

Silver is much more of a "precious" metal than the current ratio of 35-to-one would suggest.

To explain, we must first address mine supply. In 2010, the world mined approximately 736 million ounces of silver and 85 million ounces of gold.

3. The world also produced an additional 215 million ounces of silver and 53 million ounces of gold from recycled scrap.

4. Adding both together brings us 951 million ounces of silver and 139 million ounces of gold supply, for a ratio of nine ounces of silver to one ounce of gold.

Interestingly, this 9-to-one ratio is very similar to the ratio of available in-situ silver and gold reserves. The U.S. Geological Survey estimates that there are current in-situ reserves of approximately 16.4 billion ounces of silver versus 1.6 billion ounces for gold, or about a 10-to-one ratio.

5. The case for silver is even more compelling when one considers the ramifications of its dual role as both an investment and industrial metal. Last year, non-investment demand for silver (which includes industrial, photographic, and silverware demand) totaled approximately 610 million ounces.

6. This represents approximately 64% of primary supply, leaving approximately 341 million ounces to satisfy investment demand.

7. On the gold side, industrial usage totaled 13 million ounces, or about 10% of primary supply, leaving approximately 125 million ounces left over for investment demand.

8. So, after netting out the industrial usage the primary supply left over for investment demand is about 2.7 times that for gold. However, if we convert those ounces to dollars at current prices, we're left with $15 billion worth of silver available for investment versus $186 billion worth of gold, or a one-to-13 ratio of silver to gold! This means that in terms of primary supply, silver only has 8% of the capacity for investment that gold does despite having equal if not more dollars flowing into it.

Now, it's true that another potential source of supply is the very silver that investors already own - and at the right silver price these inventories of silver and gold bullion may be sold into the market to supplement any supply shortfalls. As we've noted previously, however, due to decades of underinvestment, the amount of silver bullion inventories are actually extremely small, even compared to those of gold.

9. Recent estimates suggest that reported silver bullion inventories stand at roughly 1.2 billion ounces versus 2.2 billion ounces of gold bullion, or roughly a 0.5-to-one ratio.

10. To put that amount in perspective, consider that at present there is only $52 billion worth of silver bullion/coins and over $3.3 trillion worth of gold in inventory, which could potentially be re-circulated into the market. Converting this to a ratio, you get a one-to-63 ratio of silver to gold inventories. So how is silver still priced at 35-to-one?!

All indications lead us to believe that there is now roughly an equal amount of investment flowing into silver and gold on a dollar-for-dollar basis. And although the price ratio of silver to gold has fallen substantially since the highs of 2009, our analysis strongly suggests that this ratio must move lower to restore a fundamental balance between supply and demand. Only time will tell how much lower it will go, but we would not be surprised to see it hit single digits before settling into a more sustainable equilibrium.

What the so-called silver 'experts' neglect to account for in their models and projections is that the fiat money experiment has failed. And in this context, we believe the Market has assigned world reserve currency status to gold - not USD, not EUR, and not JPY. In our opinion, gold's continued appreciation vis-à-vis every currency is assured because the great flight from fiat has only just begun. Like gold, silver also has a long monetary history, and as such, investors are now also buying silver as protection from the ravages of fiat currency debasement. Yet, when compared to gold, it is silver that offers the most attractive value proposition by virtue of the gross mispricing of its scarcity, which, we might add, has existed for many years. Thus, in our opinion, as this new bimetallic standard takes root, silver investors will continue to be justly rewarded with marked outperformance. We truly believe that this is the investment opportunity of a lifetime, and increasingly so, others are taking heed. What is clear to us is that with equal investment dollars now flowing into silver and gold, the current 35-to-one ratio is unsustainable and has only one direction to go: lower.

Keynes versus Mises

The Collectivists versus the Austrians

A basic knowledge the two major competing economic theories will help provide an understanding of the challenges faced by the global economy today. It gives an insight into why the current economic depression has occurred, what policy makers can and should do and whether they are seriously addressing the underlying causes or just addressing the most serious symptoms. Until the primary causes are accepted and dealt with, the depression will continue unabated.

The two major opposing economic theories are Keynesian economics and the Austrian School of Economics, or the Miseans.

Lord John Maynard Keynes was a British economist whose contributions have dominated modern macroeconomics and government economic policies. His thoughts gave rise to the Keynesian economics which advocate a mixed economy with a combination of private and public sector playing important roles side by side to make macroeconomic outcomes more efficient.

Born in June 1883 to an upper middle class family, he received his higher education at Eaton. His began his career at the India Office as a clerk, but soon got bored and returned to Cambridge to work on his probability theory. Keynes was not just another economist who looked at the markets and trends and predicted possible ways to avert crisis; he worked on theories to understand what motivated people to work. He studied how the rise and fall of employment impacted the spending behavior of the population, and then he came up with theories that he hoped would help economies.

His first article was published in 1909 about the global economic downturn's affect on India. In 1913 he published a book on Indian Currency and Finance, after which he was appointed to the Royal Commission on Indian Currency and Finance, where he applied economic theory to practical problems with much success. The British Government called on him during the First World War, to lend his expertise to economic matters. In this role, he persuaded the Chancellor of the Exchequer to keep specie payments (conversion of bank notes into gold) and resist the urge to suspend them.

In the 1920s, Keynes' views were not considered influential upon policy makers and academic opinion. They were termed impractical and created with clouded judgment. Keynes had said that it was not beneficial for countries like Britain to be a part of the gold standard anymore as it damaged the need for domestic policy autonomy and could make countries roll out policies encouraging deflation when rising unemployment had to be addressed.

The decision makers; the Treasury and the Bank of England disagreed. They saw a need to be part of the gold standard, believing that it would be beneficial and convinced the then Chancellor Winston Churchill re-establish it. This was not a good decision and adverse effects on the British industry and economy at the time. Keynes was left to protest against the gold standard until it was finally abandoned in 1931.

Keynes felt strongly about his anti-investment in gold theories, calling it a 'barbarous relic'. He went on to mention in one of his books that gold mining adds nothing to the wealth of the world but de-utilizes the labor involved with the process. He thought that when the amount of gold increased in the world, the world's real wealth increased, so investment in gold-mining is marketed as important but is only a pretext to dig holes in the ground looking like a sound financial investment to bankers; Keynes equated it to how leaders make an inevitable large-scale loan expenditure for wars sound like a good investment.

Keynes talked about the investment of labor and other input costs paying out handsomely due to the high prices of gold, but also stressed upon how Spain's foreign trade was destroyed by the effect on unit prices due to an abundance of precious metals. He also discussed how the preference of India to liquidate is so strong that even the addition of huge amounts of precious metals has not been able to bring down interest rates to a level that would accommodate the growth of real wealth. Keynes said that the classical view is that the impatient nature of humans keeps them poor. We like to spend money now, rather than wait for later when it would grow. However, the truth is exactly the opposite, since he attributes this situation to the high liquidity-premiums attached to money.

Looking at the international trade system, Keynes felt that its worst effect was the way countries were set against one another as each country can only maintain its employment levels if it has gold, and the only way to get this gold is by taking it from another country, which would make the employees of that country...lose their jobs.

With time criticism has come to surround Keyes' points of view on gold. Many people argue that since it is difficult for gold to be found and mined, it is difficult to obtain. This has led to its being stored for a long time and added more value, as compared to other minerals that are comparatively easier to obtain and consequently, have less value and will deplete quickly. Critics also say that Keynes has contradicted himself over and over again, from stating the investment of an economy in gold to be a waste of resources to saying that gold helps increase the real wealth of a nation. One such argument is that even though the supply of gold may spike once in a blue moon, if one looks at the bigger picture the impact is fairly low. The theory of the Indian economy's gold plight has also been contradicted; critics say that gold was hoarded by India because of its weak financial institutions and economy, so it is not a cause of the condition; rather it is a preferred solution.

Keynesian theories added to the overall economic debate, his theories about gold investment make one ask, how much do these theories really apply to my economy?

His influence today remains stronger than ever. He believed that economic forces were determined by "Animal Spirits" of individuals and that the proper way to manage economic downturns was through demand management. Enlightened rulers, acting for the good of the public could manipulate interest rates to create newfound prosperity.

Of course in such a system, the state is supreme and is allowed to take any and all actions necessary to manipulate demand and bring the economy out of whatever morass it may find itself. Never mind the fact that according to the Austrians, the reason the economy is in the doldrums in the first place is because the government was instrumental in making too much credit available to the economy. This view carried the day back in Keynes time, and eventually every country in the world found itself looking to the government to solve any and all economic "problems", no matter how serious or minor they may be.

There is much to be learned from Keynes. While many of his systems appear to be failing now, he understood that rampant hyperinflation would eventually destroy a society. But perhaps most importantly, his economic theories were an infringement upon personal liberty, elevating the state to the status of master. The individual's liberties and rights were required to take a backseat to the government's efforts to revive or save an economy.

The Austrians

Enter the Austrians. Ludwig von Mises was born in 1881 in Austria, just two years before Keynes. A university professor, Mises eventually fled to the United States to avoid Nazi persecution. His theories were built upon those of the classical economists. Also a philosopher, he postulated that the individual, when acting upon information conveyed by freely fluctuating prices, was in the best position to determine the proper course of action for both himself and the economy as a whole. This system, often referred to as lassiez-faire or libertarianism was a unique concept for its time. His system was thoroughly stated in his magnum opus, Human Action. He developed a loyal following of economists, several of whom won Nobel Peace Prizes, among them Friedrich von Hayek.

Mises believed in the classical gold standard. He wanted government to have no say in the nature, type or quantity of money. Rather, he believed that the market would create and regulate money as necessary. His famous quote, "Government is the only entity which can take a valuable commodity like paper and make it completely worthless by adding ink," which stood for the proposition that government created fiat paper money always eventually dies. Judging from current events, he certainly got that right.

The Austrians also sought to explain the existence of the business cycle. Their view was that the business cycle was created by the Keynesian cures. The cycle began when central banks seeking to spur economic growth set interest rates artificially low. The result was an appearance of prosperity, as the new money found its way into the system. The initial recipients of the newly created money would prosper most, since the inflationary effects had yet to be realized. They got the benefit of pre-inflationary money. Then an artificial boom would ensue. The cycle would then repeat itself. Businessmen, believing demand to be higher than it actually was, and that prices were cheaper than they appeared, would increase their investments. Prices would increase and they would discover that their investments were unprofitable, leading to an inevitable crash.

They felt that the high levels of debt which low interest rates foster, would lead to overleveraging and finally the inability to service the debt. Liquidation would occur, and then the cycle would be repeated, over and over again.

Most importantly, Mises believed that the day would eventually come when the system would completely breakdown, bankrupting itself. He predicted the crash of 1929 well before it occurred. His successors at the Mises Institute and other like-minded economists also predicted the

2007 real estate crash many years before it occurred. The warnings of Peter Schiff, Marc Faber, Ron Paul and many others are all over the internet (see links).

The Austrian School is not intended to be an accurate economic prediction model, but rather a system that explains why economies rise and fall and how real wealth is created. This is perhaps its most important contribution to modern economic thought. It explains that real wealth comes from savings. People give up something they want today, to save their money and hopefully earn a return tomorrow. This is called time preference and everyone engages in it to some extent. If you've ever put a dollar into an IRA or retirement account, you've given up the use of that money today, for an anticipated greater return tomorrow. If the currency unit is stable and you invest wisely, you'll get your money back with interest and the borrowing entity will invest in projects that employ people and create wealth. However, if the government is rapidly depreciating the currency, eventually people catch on and realize that savings is a net loser. They decide not to save, spending their money as fast as possible to avoid the decreased purchasing power brought about by inflation. They also increase current borrowings since today's dollars get paid back in tomorrow's depreciated dollars.

Thus a debt spiral is created, which is exactly where we now find ourselves. It leads to gambling at the bourse and the casino and reinforces the very destructive forces that society seeks to restrain. Eventually government becomes the biggest gambler of them all and pays back its debt in worthless currency thus "benefitting" from the inflationary cycle.

The Austrian School of Economics and the Business Cycle

The Austrian School of Economics and the Business Cycle theory sees business cycles as the result of excessive growth in bank credit increased by ineffective central bank policies. These include those policies that cause interest rates to remain low for a long time, which in turn cause excessive credit to be created and savings rates to be low. There are many business cycle theories:

Ricardo's business cycle theory

According to Ricardo, banks backed by the English credit bank had the right to expand credit by making loans that exceeded their gold reserves.

This created inflationary pressure. Foreigners exchanging their English bank notes for gold and removing the gold from England caused national gold reserves to decline. This led to lower gold reserves. This reduced money supply made prices fall as the loss of credit impacted business. Price deflation caused exports to rise again and eventually gold flowed into England once again.

Austrian cycle theory – interest rate manipulation

This theory states that it is not possible for inflationary forces of credit expansion to exist in today's world of hard money and free banking. The banks contain currency that represents the gold held by the bank and any bank that extended loans in excess of its reserves will soon be in trouble when other banks ask to exchange hard money for checks and bank notes issued by that bank.

Earlier, money was based on gold and silver instead of government fiat and the overall effect on economic growth was mildly deflationary. Low interest rates that accompany fiat money increase spending, reduce saving incentives, and increase investment spending which makes one think that there is more money in the system than there actually is. This leads to overheating of the economic growth and bankers need to increase interest rates to take care of inflationary pressures. This has deleterious effects on capital investment; manufacturing slows, employees are laid off, and as a result banks have to lower their interest rates and the cycle begins again.

Austrian cycle theory – Structure of production

This model is based on goods in the process model of money and time preference theory. Here, interest rates become the demand and supply for funds that can be loaned – based on whether there is supply and there is a willingness to pay for the transfer of funds for a defined time. A person who invests in land, labor, and the manufacturing inputs will want returns for the investment and the interest, which would ensure less risk in loaning the money. The longer the wait for the loan to be returned, the higher is the rate of interest associated with the goods in process.

The Hayek Triangle in this theory shows a relation between time (goods in process) and the value of the products postproduction and the interest rate associated with the process. Lowering of interest rates creates a problem as reducing consumer savings and increase in customer spending makes the economy struggle to stand back on its feet.

There have been criticisms of the Austrian business cycle theories stating that the Austrian economists give entrepreneurs far too much credit for their resource allocation but they are not able to understand the possible damages that could be caused by central bank interests. They say that there is nothing really wrong with inflation and there is no reason for the banks to hike interest rates causing a recession. In reality because there is the possibility of inflation around the corner, people stop saving and buy goods that indicate they have something of a defined value and this causes inflation to go beyond the government's monetary expansion.

Other critics question the Austrian theory connections between the central bank's interest rate policies and mal-investment practices because it seems that the boom could be entirely due to the irrationality of investors. They say that these theories only describe the business cycles but do not explain them to the level necessary to create an adequate understanding of the phenomena. The arguments is that the business cycle theories only point to actions of the reserve and central banks but not the severity of business cycles before the time of the Federal Reserve. They state that previous crashes of the economy were caused by various privately owned banks that issued paper money which could be supposedly exchanged for its gold value, but the amounts always exceeded their gold reserves.

We know that in the 1990s, when the interest rates in Austria were lowered, the world's central banks had released large amounts of gold bullion through bullion banks which reduced the price of gold and therefore investors stopped buying gold and moved to new industries. Today the market is ripe for massive investments in gold but will soon produce another bust phase, at which time it will be essential to be invested in gold.

The Austrian business cycle theory was created at a time when most borrowing was businesses from financial institutions. Times have changed now, governments get their money from inflation and taxes, or by borrowing.. This means governments are now the main borrowers. The source of economic development and growth is not consumer spending but investing in productive resources like precious metals, gold, silver and other such material that would ensure the government can save itself in case of inflation.

Current Austrian Economists and its Resurgence

The Austrian resurgence started in 1974 has been picking up steam ever since. Getting the word out on the Austrian theories about government interventionism and the free market economy is beginning to make people question the existing order. Is there really a justification for continued reckless interventions in the markets? Can the people who created the current economic crisis really get us out?

The newer generations of Austrian theorists were way ahead of the curve in their expectations of the housing crash. This made them very relevant to the current global economic malaise. The Mises Institute and other universities have helped elevate Austrian economics, and while they may not be held in the same esteem as Keynesianism by the establishment, their logic is proving irresistible to larger sections of the population at large.

After World War II, the Austrian school was virtually non-existent and completely ignored by mainstream economists. There were many reasons for this:

- The political unrest in Europe had dispersed most of the brightest minds
- Mises had been cold shouldered by the U.S. economic profession and it became difficult for him to gain his international stature back
- Hayek saw his professional eminence reduced sharply as his theories were now being considered old fashioned
- The scientific methods of Austrian economics were eclipsed by Keynesian economics

June 1974 was a milestone for the renewed acceptance of Austrian ideas. The Institute of Human Studies, led by Murray, Ludwig, and Israel hosted a conference attended by many scholars, including some who have become today's academic leaders. It was at this conference the Austrians realized that they could pursue acceptance through economic research.

Fast forward to the financial crisis of 2007-08; economists of all stripes were pointing fingers at each other. Mainstream economics came under withering criticism, as it seemed unable to explain the obvious. A vacuum of ideas was filled with theories from various schools and the new Keynesianism. The result was massive monetary and fiscal stimulus, which has proven to be a dismal failure. The stimulus provided no relief from perpetually high unemployment rates and has allowed a continual diminution in the world's standard of living. Thus, an opportunity was created for the Austrian School to fill the void and offer common sense explanations and solutions.

Mises and Hayek are credited with having revolutionized economics, being rich in a tradition that focused on the role of the dynamic market process and the nature of economization. The economists of today seem to be moving in the direction of dynamism, and Miles, Hayek, Murray, Ludwig, etc., will always be the most important influences for the economists of the future. Their theories were relevant to not only to their times but to subsequent decades and to the increasing technologically driven economies of the world.

People Never Learn–Till It's Too Late

People seem to have a basic inability or refusal to understand the world financial system's inherent weaknesses. The vulnerability of the American and Western European economies and the possibility of collapse is something few people are willing to grasp. They are stuck in a normalcy bias, which is the inability to believe that any thing other the present "normalcy" is possible. This leads them to the false conclusion that silver is a bubble and has had its run. Technical analysts and chartists, such as Robert Prechter, further reinforce this bias. Harry S. Dent's claims that we are headed for a deflationary depression where cash and the dollar will once again be king.

Their normalcy bias is based upon the Great Depression. They are predicting a repeat performance; where the money supply shrank violently and asset prices were driven down to record lows. As Mark Twain said, "History doesn't repeat, but it rhymes." And while there are many similarities between now and the 1930's, this time is in many ways quite different. In the 1930s, the Fed allowed a few large banks to fail. This led to a cascade of over 9,000 bank failures during the decade. Some cynics postulate that this was an intentional move to help improve the competitive advantage of the large banks such as Chase Manhattan Bank, Morgan Guaranty and National City. Others claim that there were anti-Semitic overtones, where the Fed deliberately allowed Jewish held banks such as the Bank of the United States in Manhattan, to fail. The late Milton Friedman had his suspicions about this.

But whatever their rationale, the Fed clearly ignored its basic mission of insuring financial stability, and refused to act as the lender of last resort. It sat idly by, while millions of Americans lost all their life savings. Banks that appeared to be solid institutions failed in record numbers, because fractional reserve banking meant that they could never have enough cash on hand to satisfy a bank run.

Finally the Fed began to grasp what they had allowed to happen; they attempted to wildly inflate the money supply. However, it was too late to reverse the damage and restore confidence in the system. While several banks can fail during relative prosperity, one large bank failure during challenging economic times can bring down the entire system. (Which is why today we have Too Big To Fail Banks). The money supply which shrank by over thirty percent in a very short time period, caused a huge deflation. There was a total loss of faith in the system; even businesses that were still credit worthy refused to borrow.

When FDR became president, he implemented "The gold confiscation" executive order and proclaimed a bank holiday to end the runs. Most people complied and surrendered their gold. The dollar was devalued, priced at $34.75 per ounce, nearly 75% more than the century long $20 per ounce. While this allowed the Fed to increase the money supply by seventy-five percent, it had little impact upon the overall economy. In fact, none of the radical interventions that FDR and his minions attempted had any long-term positive impact on the economy.

In 1939, ten years after the Wall Street Crash, Henry anti-Semitic, Jr., Secretary of the Treasury told the House Ways and Means Committee:

"We have tried spending money. We are spending more than we have ever spent before and it does not work. And I have just one interest, and if I am wrong...somebody else can have my job. I want to see this country prosperous. I want to see people get a job. I want to see people get enough to eat. We have never made good on our promises...I say after eight years of this administration we have just as much unemployment as when we started...And an enormous debt to boot!"

Rather than learning this lesson, that FDR's interventionist policies were a complete and unmitigated failure, the schools intentionally taught that he was hero who saved the country. More false words have seldom been uttered. And the lasting legacy of these New Deal programs has been, and continue to be, disastrous. In addition to becoming ever more costly failures, they spurred imitation programs and ever-larger more costly failures, such as Medicaid, Medicare and Prescription Drug Care, and now the *pièce de résistance*, ObamaCare. Which will be proven to be the most costly and economically unsound benefit program ever passed. Even if Congress should have the temerity to repeal large parts of it, they will leave or replace other portions, such as pre-existing condition coverage, covering *children* up to 26 years of age and minimum basic coverage standards, which will increase the cost of coverage and decrease the number of people who can afford it. Government programs always fail, and large government programs fail spectacularly.

Government Cannot Create Wealth—It Only Destroys It

There is a common, incorrect, belief that pervades virtually every country and every society; the notion that government has the ability to create wealth. The fact is, government is parasitic by nature. Every dollar, euro, or Yuan that flows to government is removed from the private wealth-creating sector. If it's done by taxation, openly and honestly, borrowed by selling notes and bonds, or through inflation – whereby currency units are created with no additional commodity put forth to back the new units, wealth creation is diminished.

If government overtaxes, the results can be catastrophic. We've seen countless depressions started by excessive taxation. FDR greatly prolonged the Great Depression by increasing taxes at the worst possible moment. The people who suffer the greatest injury from such actions are the poor and the middle class, the very same groups who are always most supportive of increased taxes on the wealthy. But inflation takes the greatest toll on those on fixed incomes and those who have accumulated savings held in the currency unit or in non-precious metals investments. Inflation erodes the value of savings in a very insidious manner. Banks are currently paying less than one percent interest on savings. Perhaps you can get a higher return on bank CDs and corporate bonds. But with true inflation running at a much higher rate, this means that savers are realizing a negative annual return on their savings instruments. This is also called financial repression.

It is the realization of negative real rates of return that helps undermine the entire system. People realize that they are dupes if they save in a conventional bank account or Treasury bond. As a result, they start putting their money into hard goods or into more risky instruments that they hope will enable them to earn a real positive return, or at least stay even. A vicious cycle commences, which if left unchecked, greatly damages the economy, the political system and the currency. When all faith is lost in the currency unit, hyperinflation prevails. During Weimar Germany's experiment with unlimited money printing, employees were paid twice a day to help them keep up with inflation. They would then run off to the stores and turn their fiat paper into food and other goods.

The people who caught on to this early invested every cent at their disposal into precious metals. In fact, the truly wise and forward looking, borrowed large sums of money and purchased additional precious metals and stable foreign currencies like the U.S. Dollar. Once the reichsmark collapsed, debtors were seeking out their creditors to pay back their loans in worthless currency. The creditors on the other hand were doing everything in their power to avoid their generous and willing debtors. They hoped a new monetary system would be put in place that preserved the value of their debt. This is perhaps one of the best examples how inflation perverts normal economic functioning and turns it into something out of the Twilight Zone.

Every Silver Bullet Has a Silver Lining

The Best Way to Protect Your Wealth and Your Family

Could such a sequence of events come to the United States and the modern economies of the world? Many are betting on it. Why are corporations borrowing at such an unfettered rate? By keeping the money spigot turned on high and interest rates artificially low, savvy investors the world over are taking borrowed funds and buying up the maximum amount of silver and gold possible. Normally, the author would suggest that average individuals pay down their debts and increase their savings rate. However, when high rates of inflation become an almost absolute certainty, debt repayment is the worst course of action.

Rather, we recommend a plan called Reverse Gresham's Law. Gresham's law, which was probably postulated by Copernicus, stipulates that bad money will chase out good money. For example, when the United States stopped making dimes, quarters, half dollars and dollars from silver, and instead started using nickel clad copper blanks, virtually all silver coins disappeared from circulation–thus the bad copper clad money chased the good silver money. Pre-1983 pennies are currently worth nearly three cents, two cents more than face value, due to rising copper prices. Post 1982 pennies are not worth a penny yet, as they are made of zinc, a less valuable base metal than copper. Currently, a nickel is worth nearly $.07. It is quite likely that nickels will start to disappear from circulation as well.

Reverse Gresham's Law, states that individuals facing the virtual certainty of hyperinflation or high rates of inflation should obtain and use the maximum amount of bad money possible and use it to purchase good money. Under certain conditions, borrowing as much money as you can afford to service can be a wise move. The goal is to be as invested in as much precious metal as possible. That way, if and when, there's a general fiat currency collapse, you will have preserved and possibly increased your wealth by securing the maximum amount of good money possible. There is no other way for the average middle class or upper middle class person to protect their wealth and their family.

While artwork and real estate are another means that the rich use to protect their wealth, the middle class have no such option. While no one can know how much purchasing power an ounce of silver or gold will have once the paper money regime falters, noted economic historian Bob Hoye's research including nearly 400 years of economic cycles has shown that in every credit bust/depression, the real purchasing power of precious metals increases, often by a substantial measure.

We should expect that global governments will band together in an effort to implement a world currency, at least partially backed by gold. However, this trick has been tried before. When the Euro was created, it was purported to have 15 percent gold backing. There were numerous articles published and ads placed showing gold coins or bars, making it look like the Euro was as good as gold. But it was never to be. The Swiss Franc was backed by 40 percent gold, convertible until 2000. But over time, virtually all paper supposedly back by gold fails. Inevitably, the currency winds up not being worth the paper it's printed on. It becomes impractical for the governing bodies to pay off in gold, because they always find it preferable not to limit their money printing exploits, especially by that barbarous relic, gold. Gold backing is abandoned and only a systemic financial collapse can ever bring it back.

The eventuality of a world central bank printing money for each country, with the supposed backing of gold will probably never fly. The reason is quite simple. The complete and economic devastation that will occur once the dollar and euro collapse will be all encompassing, destroying any remaining governmental credibility on the planet.

Meanwhile China has been a reverse Gresham's Law in their flight from fiat currencies. They've been buying up resource companies and producers across the globe, using their massive surpluses of fiat currencies. Their people have been allowed and encouraged to purchase gold and silver. People are dumping their Yuan for a currency that is no one else's obligation, gold and silver. The Chinese still remember the brutality of Mao, the hyperinflations of the 1930s and 1940s, the counter-revolution and Tianan-men Square. In many ways, the Chinese populace is much more skeptical and dubious about the benefits of big government and its ability to keep the economic system afloat. While China has become much wealthier in recent times and has experienced unparalleled growth rates unknown to the Western world, the people do not trust their leaders.

No doubt that China will become the dominant power in the world and probably in a short period of time. However, it is highly unlikely that the existing communist state will survive. The coming economic tsunami will touch all shores, some more than others, and while China's economy will suffer, its government won't be able to hang on. The untold truth is that many Chinese are resigning their posts in the government and the communist party. This fact is hidden in plain sight. Additionally, because rule of law is limited at best, those Chinese that manage to accumulate wealth often deposit it overseas in Singapore, Hong Kong, Switzerland, Canada, Australia and various offshore havens across the globe. Bitter past experience, watching their neighbors get dragged off in the middle of the night, has taught them that they require an insurance policy in the event they need to take sudden flight.

Silver experienced a major move in 2011. It went from under $9 per ounce in October of 2009 to $49.50 in 2011 and then pulled back violently to $27 as of the writing of this book. Such severe moves scare even sophisticated experienced investors and petrifies average middle class novices. It is the major premise of this book that while gold is always a store of value and has been used as money since time immemorial, the real wealth building opportunity is silver. However market psychology makes it impossible, or difficult at best, for investors to take the plunge. Here's an excellent exposition on why silver is the future of money.

Howard Ruff's Current Take On Silver

Howard Ruff is a well-known newsletter writer. He was a major gold and silver bug in the late 1970s and early 1980s. Unlike many, when Paul Volker stepped up and raised interest rates to twenty percent, he quickly unloaded his precious metals inventory and became a big stock investor. He was bullish on the economy and the stock market for many years. A while ago, he looked at the Federal Reserve Policy and became a born again precious metals investor. For this reason, extremely close attention should be paid to his many words of wisdom. He still publishes his investment newsletter *The Ruff Times* and while the recommendations on the report don't change much, the advice is often priceless. You can find him at *www. rufftimes.com.* We've reprinted the below silver discussion with Howard's permission.

Howard Says the average person can't afford to buy gold, so it is mostly suitable for wealthy people for investment and central banks. With silver being so much cheaper, the average person can go to his local coin dealer and buy some.

The advantages of silver over gold as an inflation hedge are numerous and need to be considered.

The silver market is much smaller, and it doesn't take as much money moving into silver as an investment to move the market up. Silver has outperformed gold dramatically over the last few years, going from $3 an ounce to nearly $50 ounce, while presently trading around $27, still a 9 fold return.

Silver is also a very important industrial metal with over 3,000 industrial uses, with new uses being added almost daily. And, the government has never seized silver, although they have seized gold. If that worries you (it doesn't worry me much), you would probably feel safer with silver rather than gold.

The government actually has no stockpile of silver to unload in effort to manipulate prices, as they do with gold. There is now more gold above ground than silver because of the silver industrial usage.

I look upon silver as money. Throughout history silver has been used more for money more than gold. Historically, silver coins became the common denominator for money in more places and more times than gold.

If you are wealthy and can afford to buy some gold, be my guest. I think you will do just fine. However, silver will outperform gold about three to one. When I receive income from my business, I set aside enough cash to take care of my normal business affairs because paper money is still a means of exchange, although it is no longer a store of value. As a means of exchange, you can conduct your normal affairs. If I have any left over, I go to my local coin dealer and buy silver.

What kind of silver should you buy?

There are American silver eagles, junk silver, and foreign silver coins that can all be bought from any coin dealer, and are also easy to sell.

The price fluctuates not just daily, but hourly. So there is always a place you could sell it.

But why would you want to sell it if the government is still inflating the currency? Hang on to your silver.

How far will silver go? Darned if I know; that's above my pay grade. All I know is that we are in a bull market, and we ain't seen nothin' yet.

I don't expect it to retreat. When I buy silver, I am just buying another form of money that I believe will prevail over paper. Where will you keep it? Any place that thieves won't be able to find it or get to it. Concealment is probably the best strategy. I wouldn't keep it in my bank safe-deposit box, just in case the government decided to change its position on silver. Right now, silver is just treated as another commodity.

The government is even manufacturing and selling silver coins. But they have no stockpile, so they have to buy on the open market just like you do. There are more people in the world who can afford to buy some silver than can afford to buy gold; thus, smaller volume will move the market up and up, and up.

Who cares about that? I don't care if it goes up. I won't sell it any time soon. This bull market will not end until the world changes its attitudes towards paper money. There is no sign of that.

Some day you might want to give it to your children or build your estate for them to inherit it. They will thank you and call your name blessed.

Is Real Estate as Good As Gold or Silver?

Many people wonder whether they should be buying real estate at this point in the economic cycle. While there is no one answer that will satisfy everyone, there are several effective approaches that can help individuals decide the best course of action. Real estate prices have declined in virtually every major metropolitan area across the country, and many areas globally. This leads investors to wonder whether they can find attractive deals at extremely low interest rates.

The real question is whether real estate prices have hit bottom, or whether the decline will continue on. Real estate may be a wise investment for those people in high tax brackets in high tax states, such as New York, California, New Jersey and Illinois. When people are faced with fifty percent combined state and local tax brackets, the government is effectively paying half of the interest and real estate taxes.

This means that if you are deciding whether to rent, you must factor in the tax subsidy and the costs of maintenance. While home ownership may no longer be the American Dream as it once was, there is a certain satisfaction that comes from owning one's own home. Own should be in quotes because until the mortgage is paid off, the bank or mortgage lender owns the property.

Additionally, when you are a renter, there's always a sense of in-security that comes with your leasehold interest. If you and your landlord have had a contentious relationship, come renewal time, your landlord might bid you adios. Or your landlord might just decide that you've done such a nice job decorating the place that he wants to live there. Only in New York City, Santa Monica and a few other choice markets, will you be entitled to an automatic right of lease renewal. In most cities, if the landlord decides that they want to rent the property to another individual after the lease has lapsed, there are no legal obstacles to his doing so.

It is possible that if you take one-year lease terms, and you rent private homes, rather than multi-family, you could be moving to a new home every year. Moving is one of the most disruptive events in a family's life. Children may have to go to new schools. Commutations may be disrupted. Shopping patterns may have to be altered. The little things that we all take for granted change. Even noted real estate bear Peter Schiff recently bought a home. He was content with the area he was living in and didn't want to go through a disruptive move. And the home was a real value, selling at less than half the price it commanded just a few years earlier. His net worth had increased so much since the crash, that the money he tied up in the home's equity was a relatively small part of his net worth, so in his case, he figured why not?

The problem is that concept of home ownership's link to the American Dream gives some individuals a false sense of security. They know that if they keep making all the payments and stay current on their real estate taxes, no one can tell them to leave (unless the government decides to build a freeway through your kitchen using eminent domain).

Another consideration is as more people fall victim to foreclosure, they will become renters and it is inevitable that rents will increase at rates above inflation. At least when you purchase a home, your interest payments will be stable for 5, 7 or even 30 years. While your taxes may increase, they will be subsidized and you may see local governments making substantial cutbacks.

How property owners will fare versus renters in the coming era of high inflation environment is another issue. Owners will have the benefit of paying back their mortgages with greatly depreciated dollars. However renters will find themselves on the opposite end of the inflation hedge. Rents will rapidly increase as inflation spirals upward. In places that have undergone hyperinflations, landlords catch on quickly and refuse to make long-term leases. Instead, they opt for six-month leases or month-to-month tenancies.

One thing is certain, now is not the time to tie up large sums of available cash in pricey real estate investments. There are areas of real estate investing that make a lot of sense for the sophisticated real estate professional. Income-producing properties, the kind where you put down very little, if any capital, and use non-recourse borrowing (they can't come after you) remains a very wise investment in certain parts of the country that are still growing. Agricultural areas such as Nebraska, Iowa and Kansas are doing extremely well because of inflated crop prices. Corn prices are going up because of the ill-advised ethanol energy subsidy program. However, all grains have been rapidly advancing in price irrespective of their suitability for alcohol refinement. In addition, North Dakota, portions of South Dakota, Montana and parts of Texas are also retaining real estate values due to expansions in the energy sector. Outside of these areas and small sub-markets scattered across the country most real estate values have been decimated.

The exception, of course, is multi-family housing and college housing. Prices are down, due to the inability of potential buyers to obtain financing and the fear of economic uncertainty. When higher inflation arrives, paving the way for possible hyperinflation, multi-family housing will take its hits like anything else. During the expected chaotic period, when there is no accepted currency or the transition is being made from the fiat currency to the next currency, rents will not be paid or will be paid in worthless currency. But so will interest payments to lenders, taxes to municipalities as well as fees to utilities.

After the initial period of chaos, there will be a currency reset. In all likelihood most debt will be forgiven or renegotiated at much lower amounts. Thus, those who are able to hold on to their multi-family properties will be well situated to maintain and later increase their wealth. This is not a suggestion to start buying up such real estate with a vengeance. Rather, if you have protected your wealth with a precious metals portfolio, you will be in a position to snap up bargains all around the globe. You need to act in a very low-key manner. People who flaunt their wealth may endanger themselves and their families. There may be the ability to buy Bentleys and Porches at just a few pennies on the dollar, but you're going to be much better off driving that beat-up Ford Explorer with 100,000 plus miles on it.

We can't emphasize enough the possible suffering that is probably going to take place. As stated less than five percent (if that) of the total population of the United States own precious metals in any form, be it stocks, certificates or actual bullion. Therefore, with the demise of the dollar and all other fiat currencies, most of the world's population will lose whatever savings and wealth they have been able to acquire. The generous government transfers or redistributive payments will end and the safety net will crumble. This will inevitably lead to great civil unrest and the breakdown of the social order. The individual has limited means and ways to prepare for this eventuality, other than acquiring self-protection items and having a security plan in place for the home, as well as purchasing precious metals.

The dissolving of social order could see many people moving to safer and more stable areas. With the price of gasoline expected to be $8 to $10 per gallon, or higher, and the availability of petroleum products scarce, it may not be practical to live in sparsely populated areas that produce neither food nor vital commodities like gold, silver or petroleum.

The Money Supply

How much money is in circulation is indirectly determined by the Federal Reserve in the United States and by the central banks of other countries. The money supply is an economic term that refers to the entire amount of money that an economy has access to at a specific time. Money has several definitions, but typically means currency that is in circulation as well as easy to access assets of depositors held in financial institutions such as commercial banks. Either the government or the central bank of the government keeps track of the country's money supply by recording as well as publishing the data. Changes in an economy's money supply can affect inflation; therefore, analysts of both the private and the public sectors monitor any reported changes.

The quantity theory of money states that a country's money supply has a comparative impact upon the country's price level. In other words, when a world economy imports silver and gold to coin money, prices of good increase. For this reason, monetary policies are created to prevent the hasty expansion of money supply. Some economic experts state that the money supply is not as much determined by the country's central bank as it is by the actual state of the economy. Many economists feel that the central bank's regulation of the money supply is a meager attempt to control inflation, as there are many other better ways to maintain price levels.

Money is a relative term, but is essentially used as a means of value that can be exchanged for goods or debt settlement. Narrow monetary aggregates are defined as liquid assets, or those that can be spent easily, such as currency. Broad monetary aggregates are assets that are harder to liquidate, such as certificates of deposit. Narrow monetary aggregates are controlled by and greatly affected by a government's monetary policies, while they less affect the broad monetary aggregates.

There are ways to classify the various types of money from the narrowest measures to the broadest. The "M" classifications range from M0 on the narrow end of the spectrum to M3, which is the broadest. The "M" designations can vary by country, but there are some steadfast rules. For instance, MB is the label for an economy's monetary base. This base is typically the most liquid of the money supply and is the base upon which the country's other money forms are created. MZM is the term for money that has zero maturity.

M0 is a classification that for the United States Federal Reserve includes all currency that is in circulation, such as notes and coins. This is currency that is not held in the Federal Reserve Banks, but that is in current circulation and might be held in commercial banks. In the United Kingdom, the M0 classification also includes bank reserves, so in that economy M0 refers to the monetary base instead of MB. In the United States, M1 designates the bank reserves separately.

M2 refers to money and any close substitute for money. M2 is a term used by economists when they need to calculate all of the money in circulation while working to explain different conditions of the monetary economic system. M2 typically calculates all of the M1 designation plus short-term deposits, with short-term being defined as up to one year. Economic experts use M2 as a way of forecasting inflation since it is a key indicator of the economic state.

M3 is a designation that is no longer documented, but some private organizations still maintain estimates. M3 refers to all of the currency in circulation, traveler's checks, demand deposits, checkable deposits, savings deposits, and all time deposits. M4 is a classification that refers to all of the M3 designations plus deposits place in the country by foreigners as well as other government's ministries.

The money multiplier is the rate determined by a ratio of the M2/M0 classifications and determines the required reserve percentage that all commercial banks must maintain of their depositor's money. The reserved money is typically held in cash and stored within the bank's vault or deposited at one of the country's central banks. The reserve ratio affects monetary policy by controlling and manipulating interest rates on borrowed money by regulating how much money is available to be loaned. Any bank that holds more in reserve than required, is said to be holding excess reserves.

Central banks in the Western part of the world seldom change the required reserve as it can cause liquidity problems for banks that hold a low amount of reserved cash. Most monetary policy adjustments are made instead by selling and buying stocks issued by the government. The United States does not adjust the reserve requirement very often, as there is a large gap of time that occurs between the change and effect it has on inflation. In some countries reserve requirements are adjusted regularly. The People's Bank of China fights inflation by changing their reserve requirements and they raise the requirements frequently.

As the required amount of reserves a bank must hold increases, the amount of money that is available to loan out is reduced, thereby lowering the creation of money and maintaining the value and purchasing power of the money in still in circulation. The effect on an economy's money supply can be shown in the formula: $MS = Mb * mm$, where MS is the money supply; Mb is the monetary base; and mm is the money multiplier. $mm = (1 + c) / (c + R)$, where c is the rate people hold onto the cash rather than deposit it; and R is the reserve requirement.

In the United States, the liquidity ratio, or reserve requirement percentage is separated into rules based upon the size of the bank and typically only effect transaction accounts such as checking accounts. Time deposit accounts including savings accounts, CDs, or foreign company or government deposit accounts are treated separately. For instance, banks that have up to $10.7 million USD do not have a minimum requirement amount. These banks are regulated by the capital requirement ration instead. Banks with between $10.7 million USD and $55.2 million must hold back 3% for reserve. Financial institutions with more than $55.2 million USD are required to hold back 10%. For the time deposit accounts, banks are required to hold only 1% to satisfy the fractional reserve requirement. If a bank happens to fall below their required amount of reserve by way of unexpected cash withdrawal demand for example, the bank can take out a short-term loan with either the Federal Reserve Bank or any other bank that has an excess amount of reserves. These loans are normally for a lifetime of 24 hours or less.

In the United Kingdom, The Bank of England has no minimum requirement of reserves, relying instead on a voluntary system of reserve ratios. While this means that theoretically, a bank would not have to hold any money in reserve, but in actuality, the average amount held in the banking system across all of the United Kingdom is over 3%. Other countries with no mandatory reserve requirement are Australia, Canada, New Zealand, and Sweden. Countries with a higher than 10% requirement include Croatia with 14%, Costa Rica and Malawi with 15%, Hong Kong with 18%, Brazil and Tajikistan with 20%, and Suriname and Lebanon with a whopping 25% and 30% respectively. Some countries have held widely varied liquidity ratios, such as in 1978, when the country of Turkey had an astounding 62.7% cash reserve ratio, but reduced it to 18% in 1998.

Bank runs occur when a number of customers of a bank demand a withdrawal of their deposits at the same time. Most often, this happens because the customers believe that the bank is subject to collapse or has already been bankrupted. As a bank run progresses, it becomes a sort of self-fulfilling prophecy in which the more money people withdraw, the more insolvent the bank becomes, which leads to yet more people fearing the collapse of the bank and withdrawing their money as well. These abrupt withdrawals by a bank's depositors can destabilize the bank, forcing it is some cases to file bankruptcy because of the bank run itself.

Financial crises such as banking panics or systemic banking crises can occur when a bank run is widespread, leading to the extensive number of banks suffering the devastating effects of large-scale demand. When several banks are wiped out, an economic recession can happen, leading to overwhelming destruction. The Great Depression was in fact caused in large part by large runs on banks and the costs to a government for economic cleanup can be massive.

There are many ways to prevent a bank run, such as a suspension of withdrawals for a short period; the borrowing of money from a bank of last resort, bank regulation by the government, and deposit insurance like that provided by the United States Federal Deposit Insurance Corporation. Sometimes these measures work effectively, especially if bank customers are fearful of losing their money due to factors such as bank reorganizations.

Economic bubbles can lead to bank runs, like the first recorded economic (speculative) bubble called Tulip mania in the 1630s Dutch Golden Age. Contract prices of tulip bulbs sharply increased when they were first introduced, with some bulbs being sold for as much as 4200 florins. Considering the average skilled artisan only earned approximately 300 florins a year, tulip bulbs were priced a great deal higher than their intrinsic value. Tulips were valued for their luxuriousness, rarity, and symbol of status, but when the prices collapsed, many investors were ruined.

Speculation also ruined the South Sea Company's stock. The British company received exclusive rights to trade with the South American colonies for the price of the national debt of England. While the company thought this to be a grand exchange, the price of company stock rose significantly over the course of just one year and caused widespread interest in trading, even amongst the lower classes. When the stock prices fell, many of the people who had borrowed money in order to buy stocks found themselves bankrupt.

During the 1930s the Great Depression caused financial devastation across the entire globe. Of all the financial crises of the 20th century, the Great Depression was the worst. October 29, 1929, referred to as Black Tuesday, resulted in many people who never traded in stocks feeling the effects. Bank runs occurred through 1933, and became even more devastating as scandals in New York and Los Angeles financial institutions were uncovered.

While some countries began to recover within a few years, others experienced the ill effects of the depression until the start of the Second World War. In the Hollywood movie, *It's a Wonderful Life*, the film's hero fights to maintain his Building and Loan company, despite the large number of depositors trying to withdraw their money.

Bank runs and panics have caused many recessions in the United States, and therefore many commercial banks have policies in place to prevent the damage to the country's economy. In the 1980s and 90s the Savings and Loan crisis occurred when the Tax Reform Act of 1986 was passed, effectively diminishing the value of many real estate investments which the Savings and Loan companies held on their books. In 2007, a financial crisis of global scale was precipitated by plummeting real estate interest rates, which caused a housing price bubble.

A bank run can lead to a systemic bank crisis by causing a domino effect of banking collapses as more and more bank customers fear further bouts of banking failure and thereby create a self-fulfilling prophecy of more banking failure with their requests to pull out all of their money.

Zombie banks are essentially financial institutions that have less than zero net worth, but are allowed to maintain operations because their government is providing them with credit support. Silent runs can then occur if investors and depositors start to worry about a country's ability to support their central bank, causing a rise in the cost to fund zombie banks. In this manner the zombie banks bleed benefits from healthy banks by selling its assets and rolling over liabilities at higher interest rates.

Bankruptcy is a term that refers to a business or person being unable to repay their financial debts to creditors. Most often, the debtor initiates a bankruptcy, but in some cases, a creditor can petition the court for an involuntary bankruptcy or restructuring in an effort to recoup at least a portion of what they are owed.

Private moneylenders are typically small businesses who make loans to people who are likely to be turned down by traditional financial institutions due to poor credit or inadequate collateral. As the risk of default is much higher on these loans, the interest rates charged to borrowers is much higher, sometimes as much as 100% and 400% annual percentage rate. Private moneylenders commonly make small, unsecured short-term loans, collecting their payments weekly. Even though the costs are very high, these loans are popular with people who are unable to obtain financing any other way.

Hard moneylenders offer short-term loans that are backed in most cases by real estate. Higher interest rates are also the norm with these types of loans as most of them do not require credit approval and therefore have a higher default rate. The typical ratio of lending is up to 65% of the property value. Many states in the U.S. have regulations that govern these types of institutions in order to protect consumers.

Hyperinflation

Inflation is the condition of rising prices of consumer goods and services at a continual and increasing rate caused by growing amounts of available credit and circulating currency, in spite of a lower proportion of goods and services available for sale. When the price levels rise, the same amount of currency begins to provide for less and leads to a wearing down of purchasing power and a loss of value at the international exchange level. The annual percentage change of the general price index or Consumer Price Index is the yearly indicator of the inflation rate.

Inflation can be both beneficial and detrimental to an economy. On the negative side, the real value of currency can decrease over time, leading to less investing and saving and potential hoarding of goods by consumers. On the positive side, central banks such as the Federal Reserve Bank will be able to offer lower interest rates and other incentives to encourage investments and savings. Inflation has no effect on the real value of items that are of non-monetary value.

There are many theories about the creation and development of inflation. The original theory proposed by historian and philosopher, David Hume, in the 18th century says that prices will go up whenever the supply of money is increased. In the middle of the 20th century, economist Milton Friedman stated that in order to maintain steady prices, a government needed to raise the supply of money in equal relation to the growing economy.

John Maynard Keynes, the famous British economist who created macroeconomics and advocated government run economies believed in income determination, which asserts that inflation occurs when demand is greater than supply. He believed that government could gain control of inflation by raising or lowering interest rates, effectively managing the levels of taxation and consumer spending. Another theory, called the cost-push theory says that inflation is caused by a cycle of workers demanding a higher wage. This leads to employers raising the cost of the goods and services they provide in order to pay that higher wage, which in turn leads the employees to ask for yet more money in an effort to afford the higher priced goods and services. A final economic theory, called the structural theory says that when a developing country begins to import more than they export it pushes down their currency's value on an international scale and effectively leads to higher prices on an internal level.

Overall, most economists agree that inflation rates increase due to a correlating increase in the money supply. Small levels of inflation rate increase might only be caused by an enhanced demand for a specific good or service or perhaps due to lowered availability of specific goods or services, but sustained inflation rate growth is generally attributed to an economy's money supply increasing faster than their rate of growth. A rate of slow and steady inflation is best for an economy as it can make the effect of an economic recession less severe as well as allow labor markets to recover more quickly after a slump.

Hyperinflation is inflation that is out of control within a single economy and does not typically affect foreign currencies or price levels. The affected economy's local currency loses value at alarming rates and the cycle of hyperinflation is perpetuated by more money being printed. Hyperinflation can be caused by an increasing money supply, but the effects are doubled, as consumers don't wish to hold onto the hyper-inflated money long enough for it to be converted into something of non-monetary value, which would effectively end the loss of real value.

Hyperinflation occurs most often as a result of wars, political turmoil, social disturbances, or overactive amounts of currency exchange bidding. The International Accounting Standards Board defines hyperinflation as an inflation rate that culminates in a rate of 100% over a three-year period, but Philip Cagan, the American economist, defines hyperinflation as a monthly rate of 50% inflation.

The cause of hyperinflation is the same as basic inflation, but because of the disproportionate ratio of money to available goods, people lose confidence in the value of money and increase their spending, which in turn ramps up the level of pricing. Attempts to stimulate the economy by printing more paper money often fails, as it is devalued before the money is even printed.

Many countries have experienced hyperinflation. China was the first country to use fiat currency and has historically suffered from bouts of hyperinflation. During the Yuan Dynasty (later half of the 13th century and first half of the 14th century), a large amount of paper money was printed in an effort to finance wars, but the consequent hyperinflation was a contributing factor in the dynasty's fall. Marco Polo travelled extensively throughout China and created a great interest in all goods from China. His cartography, along with his published manuscripts encouraged many travelers to try to reach the Far East by sea in a westward direction, including Christopher Columbus.

Unfortunately, the collapse of the Mongol Empire was a leading factor in political unrest. All of the cultural aspects of the empire as well as the region's economic stability were affected. The Silk Road was taken over by Turkic tribes, which later became the Ottoman Empire. The Yuan Dynasty was overthrown in 1368, leading to the Ming Dynasty's policies of economic isolationism. With the advent of gunpowder, territorial states in Europe were integrated and mercantilism was increased, but in the East, trade declined rapidly, and by 1400, the Silk Road was effectively closed.

After the end of World War II, China was taken over by the communist party in 1949 after a long and drawn out war between internal revolutionaries and communists. By 1948, China was in the throes of the worst hyperinflation in their history. It wasn't ended until the communist government revalued the renminibi (official currency of the People's Republic of China).

During the French Revolution from 1789 to 1799, social unrest and political turmoil was far-reaching, spanning across France and spilling into other parts of Europe. The collapse of the absolute monarchy in France created a societal transformation of epic proportions leading to the age of Enlightenment. The events that led to the French Revolution included serious economic factors such as hunger caused by years of lower than average grain harvests leading to sharp increases in bread prices. Conditions were worsened by widespread transportation issues, which made the food shipments from farms to the populated cities very difficult.

King Louis XVI came to power when the financial crisis was thoroughly underway. France was effectively facing bankruptcy as a result of the financial strain of paying for previous wars, such as France's participation in the American Revolutionary War. The national debt grew and France's financial system was not sufficiently robust to recover from, largely as a result of their faulty taxation system. The country forced most of the tax burden on the lower classes and allowed the clergy and nobles many exemptions. When the Comptroller, Jacques Necker stated that the country must reform its tax system he was fired. The next Comptroller, Charles Alexandre de Calonne soon found himself in the same situation as Necker when he proposed sweeping taxation changes.

In 1795, the franc was established as the metallic currency of France, replacing the livre. However, the decline in circulation of francs led to an increase in the printing of paper money, the assignat. Originally, the assignat was only a bond, but later was made the legal tender of France. The situation was not resolved until after Napoleon seized power and reformed the entire tax and legal system of the country.

In more recent times the government of Zimbabwe has experienced widespread hyperinflation due to the collapse of their financial economy. Currently, Zimbabwe is tormented by the world's second worst case of hyperinflation in history, just behind Hungary in 1946. In 1998, Robert Mugabe, the president of Zimbabwe who is well known as a voice against white-minority government rule, initiated land reforms that aimed to reclaim white owned farmland, giving it back to black farmers. This redistribution of land and assets caused food production and income from food exports to plunge. Mugabe was forced to print more paper money in ever larger denominations.

By 2004, Zimbabwe's inflation rate was 624%, rising to 1,730% by 2006. Despite the revaluation by the Reserve Bank of Zimbabwe to a ratio of 1,000 ZWD per second ZWD, yearly inflation rates were rising, and by mid 2007, the inflation rate had risen to 11,000%. Within one month, the inflation rate had soared to an unbelievable rate of 2,200,000%. By summer of 2008, the ZWD value was around 688 billion to 1 USD, or 688 trillion of pre-2006 ZWD dollars.

In 2008, the Zimbabwe government revalued their dollar, but the inflation rate was well over 11,000,000%, with the annual inflation rate hitting 231,000,000% and the average prices were doubling within 18 days at a time. Rates were not officially published for a time after this, leading some economists to estimate those rates. Estimation of the inflation rate during the autumn of 2008 were thought to be around 80 billion percent monthly, which meant that prices had to be doubling within 25 hours, but these estimates could not be proven.

Argentina has recently been reporting a single digit inflation rate, but from the 1970s throughout 2010, Argentina had been experiencing the world's third worst inflation rate with an average of 215.46%. The highest inflation level peaked in the spring of 1990 at a record-breaking 20,262.80% compared to a negative inflation rate in early 1954 of -7%. In 2002, Argentina's currency, the peso, was devalued and prices for consumer goods such as eggs and televisions rose by 100% or higher.

Argentina's problems began in 1947 when leftist Juan Peron became president, but did not reach endemic proportions until 1974 as a result of the government's devaluation of the currency and an extreme (175%) rise in the price of oil. Public opinion was that the government caused inflation as a means of creating pandemonium.

The peso's value fell by 70% and the prices of imported goods rose significantly, but fortunately, the public utilities prices were frozen to stem inflation. While the hyperinflation of the 1980s and 90s had long since passed, 2002 was still a year of suffering as the country experienced a near 20% unemployment rate and stagnant wages. The largest denomination of the peso was 1,000 in 1975, but within a year, the highest denomination was 5,000 pesos. By 1981, it had reached 1,000,000 and by 1992, the value of 1 current peso was worth 100,000,000,000 pre-1983 pesos.

The economic crisis in Argentina reached its peak between 1999 to the early 2000s. The domestic currency convertibility measure of 1990 was designed to protect the domestic currency from creditors refusing Argentine pesos as payment. Unfortunately, corruption was rampant within the government and public debt was growing. By 1999, the country had entered a recession and ended with an economic collapse in 2002.

Israel is another country that is recovering from astounding rates of inflation, with current reports of a steady and respectable 4.3% rate. Between 1984 and 2004, rates soared as high as 486.23% in autumn 1984 and plummeted to a -2.74% in the spring of 2004. From the early 1970s and into the 1980s, there were periods of hyperinflation. Where consumer prices rose only 13% in 1971, they had risen 445% by 1984. People in Israel began hoarding non-monetary items such as phone tokens so that their value would remain stable.

At the outset of the inflationary period, Israel's government decided to raise the wages of workers to keep up with the rate of inflation. In order to do this, they expanded the money supply. While this did in fact make the workers feel the pinch of inflation less, the increased money supply only added to the cyclic effects. As workers made more money, prices went up. By the mid 1980s, government leaders had developed an effective plan of economic stabilization, which started with freezing prices of most products. Within a year, the inflation rate was cut in half, and by 1986 the inflation rate was down to double digits, at 19%.

Since governments often print extra money from their central banks as an initial stopgap method to deal with inflation, it has created some odd paper money denominations. When smaller notes became worthless it was common practice to print larger denominations of the currency, resulting in some extremely high valued banknotes. For example, during the height of Hungary's hyperinflation in 1946, the Hungarian National bank issued a note worth 100 quintillion pengõ. Their inflation rate at that time was the largest in history, at 41.9 quadrillion percent, but has now been beaten by Zimbabwe's annual inflation rate of 89.7 sextillion.

Gold is a precious, shiny metal that in its pure state is bright yellow. Highly valued for its chemical elements, it was used in products such as jewelry and coins long before people recorded history. Gold is the basis for many monetary systems throughout the world, replaced largely by the fiat monetary system only within the last century. In addition to its symbolic uses it has practical uses in fields such as dentistry and electronics. Although gold is not the monetary standard of the world any longer, many people still invest in gold.

Gold is measured in troy weight and grams. When other metals have been alloyed with the gold, the terms karat or carat are used to describe the amount of pure gold in the product, with 24 carats indicating pure gold. Market trading now sets the price of gold, and The London Gold Market Fixing Ltd. is the company responsible for setting the benchmark price twice each day for the global gold market. Each day at 10:30 am and 3 pm GMT, the gold fix is determined for the U.S. dollar, the British pound sterling, and the Euro.

Silver is also a precious metal that has a higher conductivity of electricity than any other element, as well as a higher thermal conductivity of any other metal. Silver has long been used in making jewelry, eating utensils, and currency. Silver is also used in the fields of electricity and dentistry. Many countries have used silver as the basis of valuing money, but the discovery of large silver deposits in the American Continent in the late 19th century caused an exchange to the gold standard by most countries by the start of the 20th century. Many countries have now replaced the gold standard with the fiat system of currency.

Gold and silver are experiencing resurgence in popularity as many governments and central banks have started to buy up gold and silver again. While countries work to devalue their own currencies in an effort to gain trade advantages, gold remains steady with rising value, making it easy to see why gold and silver have long been popular currency. Despite changes in the value of both gold and silver, they retain most of their value over time, unlike paper currency. For example, at the beginning of the 20th century, one U.S. dollar would buy 14 loaves of bread, but will now only buy one loaf or less. Inflation has affected the dollar tremendously, but one ounce of gold will still buy an average set of clothing, just as it has since the 1300s.

Central banks have long understood the value of gold, and to a lesser extent silver, by lining their reserves with the precious metals. Countries with foreign exchange reserves and large trade surpluses have been increasing their reserves of gold since early 2010 in order to gain an advantage over their competition. One of the possible theories of gold's increased popularity is the rumor that it and silver may play a major part in the international system of currency.

Since the early days of American history gold prices have held the fascination of gold collectors, regardless of its use as a basis of monetary systems. It is important to consider first the difference between official and market prices before evaluating the changes in prices over the years. The official price of gold is determined by the gold's fineness and weight. Due to the gold-coin standard, there is a difference between gold's official price and its mint price. The difference was originally made of mint charges, or essentially the profit paid to the agency that minted the coin. The market price of gold is determined by the market, but is heavily influenced by the official price, as individuals can opt to trade with the monetary power of a government rather than strictly within the market. In the U.S., the Resumption Act of 1875 eliminated mint charges. While in Britain, there were no mint charges, but the mint could refuse gold bullion that required measures to refine its quality before minting.

United States gold prices from 1786 through 1791 were $19.39 per ounce, but that priced dropped to $19.39 per ounce from 1792 to 1833. The price of gold surpassed the $20 mark in 1834 and while it fell by 2 pennies in 1836, remained relatively constant for one hundred years. As the U.S. banned privately held gold reserves in 1933, the exchange rate was $20.37, but raised and fixed at $35.00 per ounce soon after. The price continued steady until the ban was lifted in the early 1970s, when $42.22 became the going rate per ounce of gold. Throughout history it is important to note that wide fluctuations occurred during these years, but the reported price is the closing price at the end of stated year.

Silver prices in the U.S. have been affected throughout history by its use as a measure of monetary value as well as its popular use in industry. According to experts, there is only about $4 billion dollars of mined silver left in the world and this greatly affects the price. In the late 1700s and through 1813, silver cost on average $1.293 U.S. dollars. From 1814 to 1816, prices fluctuated from $1.477 to $1.323 before settling back into $1.293 in 1817 and remaining steady until 1837 when it reached $1.350. Prices stabilized in 1838 to $1.292 and then in 1862 fell to $1.709. With the exception of the staggering increase that occurred in 1864, bringing silver prices to a historic $2.939, silver remained well under the $2 mark. In 1887 silver prices per ounce dropped down to less than $1 U.S. dollar with only a brief reprieve in 1890 and again in 1918 and 1919 with rates as high as $1.336 per ounce. Not until the 1960s did silver prices recover to surpass the $1 dollar mark, and in 1979, prices broke all records with an astonishing $21.793 price per ounce. This was the period of time that the Hunt brothers from Texas were attempting to corner the market, but went bankrupt when regulations prevented investors from borrowing in order to buy silver. After a slight dip to $16.393 in 1980, silver returned to its relatively lower price, where it has remained until recently.

Many times throughout history, bans on the private ownership of gold have occurred in an effort to revive a stagnant economy. During the Great Depression, U.S. President Franklin D. Roosevelt banned the hoarding of gold bullion, gold certificates, and gold coins by citizens of the United States. Known as Executive Order 6102, the ban became effective in 1933, just in time to stem the outward flow of gold holdings from the Federal Reserve. The order required all citizens to turn in all of their private gold holdings with the exceptions of small amounts by the beginning of May 1933 to the Federal Reserve.

The price of $20.67 per troy ounce of gold was established for an exchange rate. Only people who worked in certain industries were allowed to retain their stores of gold. Individuals were permitted to own up to $100 worth of gold coins, or five troy ounces. In an effort to raise money, the U.S. Treasury increased the price of gold to $35 per troy ounce and used the profits to provide for the Exchange Stabilization Fund.

President Dwight D. Eisenhower further restricted private gold ownership in 1961 by restricting American's gold holdings overseas. President John F. Kennedy furthered the Eisenhower ban by completely disallowing foreign-held gold bullion and required all citizens who held their gold overseas to sell it immediately. By 1971, the United States was experiencing a continued loss of value on the dollar and gold holdings were diminishing, meaning that the U.S. was only able to cover approximately one-third of dollars held in the central banks of foreign governments. President Nixon, fearing those central banks would demand an exchange of dollars to gold; he stated that the U.S. would be unable to exchange U.S. dollars for gold as of August 15, 1971.

As the dollar faced continuing devaluation, the price of gold on the private market was nearing $90 per ounce. In the spring of 1973, all ties of gold to the dollar were cut. The U.S. Congress also gave the President discretion to allow private gold ownership as long as such ownership would not affect the international financial position of the United States. While he was President, Richard Nixon did not choose to act on it, and President Gerald Ford repealed the gold ownership ban in 1974. The ban on private gold ownership in the U.S. was officially ended after a reign of forty years, bringing about instant increase in the price of gold.

By 1980, gold had reached a historical price of $850 per ounce, which was in large part due to political unrest in the Middle East, with Russian involvement in Afghanistan as well as the revolution in Iran. High inflation rates and oil prices encouraged investors to buy up gold.

Since then prices have dropped and remained relatively steady in the $300 range before beginning a climb upward again in recent years.

Paul Volcker served as President of the Federal Reserve Bank in New York from 1975 through most of 1979, leaving only for the post of Chairman of the U.S. Federal Reserve, which he held for eight years. Appointed by President Jimmy Carter and reappointed by President Ronald Reagan to the office of Chairman, Paul Volcker also served as Chairman of the President's Economic Recovery Advisory Board to current President Barack Obama, from February 2009 until February 2011. Volcker is considered the man who finally stemmed the widespread effects of high inflation and low economic growth, which had created stagflation in the U.S. economy. In 1981, the inflation rate was 13.5%, just two years later it was only 3.2%.

The way that Volcker effectively ended inflation in the U.S. was to raise the interest rate on federal money loaned by private banks to other private banks. Volcker raised the rates from the average rate of 11.2% in 1979, to a staggering 20% in the summer of 1981. The prime rate reached 21.5% that same year. When private depository institutions fall below their required reserve amounts, borrowing money from other banks that have an excess reserve allows the bank to maintain its required reserve fund. This money is typically paid back within 24 hours. The high interest rates affected more than just the banks themselves, including sectors like farming and construction.

Protests against Volcker and his methods resulted in some farmers actually creating a blockade around the Eccles Building where the Federal Reserve Board is located. The Reagan Administration fired Paul Volcker in 1987, stating that he was less than adequate at deregulation, but many people in the government gave him sole credit for the drop in inflation rates.

Paul Volcker sounded off repeatedly during his stint as economic advisor to President Obama, saying that the banks need to be regulated in a stricter fashion, called for many of the nation's largest banks to be broken apart and prevented from engaging in risky financial activities. In January of 2010, President Obama introduced "The Volcker Rule", in honor of his regulatory suggestions.

As of mid-April 2011 gold has reached the record high price of $1,503.48 per ounce, bringing with it a record breaking high for silver prices as well. While the price of silver inched toward the $50 mark during the last week of April, gold neared $1520 per ounce. These high prices haven't been seen in the silver market since the days of the Hunt brothers, and many were worrying about the result.

Many investors, both private and business, have been buying up silver and gold as a way to circumvent potential global financial crises that have led to inflation. When the ratings agency of Standards & Poor issued a downgraded rating for U.S. debt, a great number of investors dumped their U.S. Treasury bonds and invested heavily in precious metals instead. With a slowdown of the global economy and worries about inflation, gold and silver investments are continually looking more attractive.

As the outlook on U.S. government debt shifted from stable to negative, the U.S. dollar is now becoming even weaker as both foreign and domestic investors look for sanctuary. Add on concerns about sovereign debt in Europe and inflation rates that continue to grow on a global scale, and many people are finding it has simply never been a better time to invest in the precious metals.

The political turmoil facing Northern Africa and the countries of the Middle East has only increased concerns in the world of global finance.

Vietnam—The Economy of the Not Too Distant Future

Gold, Gresham's Law & the Dong

Ben Traynor. What happens when people actively shun their official currency...?

Governments are often tempted to live beyond their means. Today, that means national debts and quantitative easing. But a few hundred years ago, it meant debasing coinage.

Silver and gold coins would be 'clipped' – with a tiny quantity of their metal shaved off the edge every time they passed through government hands – or they would be minted with a lower precious metal content than their face value stated. This would enable the monetary authorities to produce more coins for the same amount of bullion, increasing the government's spending power in the marketplace.

The net result was that coins with identical face values did not necessarily hold the same commodity value. And this often led to a rather interesting phenomenon. When people knew there were both 'good' and 'bad' coins floating around, they tended to spend the bad and hang onto the good. Before long, all the good money disappeared into hoards. The only money in circulation was bad money.

This is known as Gresham's Law, named after the sixteenth century financier Sir Thomas Gresham. In its most simple form, Gresham's Law is often stated as "bad money drives out good money", and its no mere historical curiosity. Gresham's Law is alive and kicking today in many countries all around the world.

Vietnam provides a textbook example. Vietnam's economy uses three different forms of money today. There is the official currency, the Vietnamese Dong. There is also the U.S. Dollar, which Vietnamese people tend to trust a bit more. And then, there is gold.

Gold is a big deal in Vietnam. The average Vietnamese spends more of each unit of income on gold than anyone else on Earth. Total gold buying amounted to 3.1% of GDP last year. (By comparison, private gold purchases amounted to 2.5% of India's GDP, while China's were a mere 0.4%.)

All told, an estimated 500 tons of gold – over $24 billion worth – is hoarded away in Vietnam, reckons Huynh Trung Khanh, deputy chairman of the Vietnam Gold Business Council. It's hidden in mattresses and buried in the garden. But gold is not just a store of value in Vietnam. It is also used as a medium of exchange. Which is why, in the day-to-day sense, it also functions as money.

In Vietnam you can put gold in a bank and earn interest. People quote house prices in gold, and pay for them with tael gold bars - each bar weighing approximately 1.2 troy ounces. This makes sense when you consider that Vietnam is a largely cash society. A single property can cost up to 4 billion Vietnamese Dong. That's a lot of paper to count and check.

But if the Vietnamese love their gold, the same cannot be said of the country's central bank. In recent years the State Bank of Vietnam (SBV) has issued several Decrees and Circulars whose combined effect–whether by accident or design–has been to undermine gold's official monetary role:

June 2008 - Gold imports banned (though smuggling continues).

March 2010 - All gold trading floors closed.

October 2010 - SBV issues Circular 22, banning banks from dealing with manufacturers and traders of gold bars.

May 2011 - SBV bans all gold lending activity.

The latest decree is an attempt to end the practice of banks paying interest on gold (presumably in the hope that people will substitute their gold for paper). Up to now, banks have offered interest on physical gold deposits. They sell the metal on, lend the proceeds as Dong loans and buy an equivalent amount of gold forward from an international bullion bank.

This has been a profitable activity for the banks because domestic interest rates have tended to be high enough to cover both the forward rate and the rate they were paying the depositor. Essentially it was a carry trade; borrow gold (from depositors) cheaply, lend at a higher rate.

As of May 1, however, banks will be forbidden to undertake any gold lending activities. And from May 2013 they will have to stop paying interest on gold deposits.

This latter measure may largely be moot by then. As you might expect, with the lending channel blocked, there's no money in it anymore. Gold deposit rates have already fallen sharply.

So why all the rule changes? Well, the authorities see gold as a "bad influence" – a destabilizing factor in an already messy economic picture. Consider the following problems afflicting Vietnam:

1) A Large and Growing Trade Deficit - The trade deficit in 2010 was around 12% of GDP. Even worse, it grew wider in the first four months of the year.

2) Rising Inflation - Latest figures from Vietnam's General Statistics Office show CPI inflation at a whopping 17.5%, despite a supposedly tight monetary policy.

3) A Falling Currency - The Dong has been devalued six times since June 2008. Most recently was February 11 this year, when it fell 8.5%.

Sound at all familiar? The way the central bank sees it, the propensity of the Vietnamese to buy gold also makes these problems worse. Gold imports exacerbate the trade deficit (it has no domestic mine output). Buying gold thus weakens the Dong, which puts upward pressure on inflation. Gold (and indeed Dollar) ownership also undermines the SBV's monetary policy, since its interest rates only apply to the Dong.

But you can hardly blame the Vietnamese people for buying and hoarding gold. Not when you remember that Viet inflation is running at 17.5%. In this regard, gold ownership is a direct consequence of economic conditions. The only way the SBV could provide Vietnamese with an incentive to save in Dong would be to raise the nominal interest higher than inflation, and thus provide a decent real rate of return. But this would mean rates of around 20% at least. Not only would this hit the domestic economy hard, it would almost certainly cause the Dong to appreciate, which would make the trade deficit even worse.

Unable, therefore, to directly incentivize people to hold paper money, the authorities have resorted instead to marginally disrupting gold's monetary function. But this won't work. People will still prefer to hold gold because the Dong is failing to fulfill one of the core functions of money. It is a terrible store of value.

That is why the Vietnamese continue to hoard "good" money (gold) while passing the bad stuff around – just as Gresham's Law predicts.

Vietnam is stuck in an inflation-devaluation cycle. Ordinary people do not trust its paper currency, and sell it for something better. This reduces its value against other currencies. It also reduces its value against goods and services, which takes the form of rising consumer prices. All of which serves to make the Dong even less popular...

Could this vicious cycle ever strike the U.S. Dollar, British Pound, or the Euro? Maybe it's already begun. Gold and silver prices have risen strongly over the last decade in all those currencies, and especially versus the Dollar so far in 2011. This tells us that many Westerners – just like the Vietnamese – are keen to swap their paper for metal.

If the Dollar and its paper cousins continue to leak value, savers will increasingly prefer "good money" like gold and silver. After all, it's Gresham's Law.

What Happens when Money Dies?

The death of money. Walk down the street. Take a good look around. Most of the people you encounter cannot conceive of a dollar that has lost its perceived value. It is unfathomable to them. They know something is wrong with the economy, but they are content to rely on the fallacious reasoning of the mainstream economic prevaricators, led by Nobel laureate Paul Krugman and people like tax cheat Treasury Secretary Timothy Geithner and fully discredited Fed Chief Benjamin Bernanke. The majority of the world's population has abdicated its role as a check on the unfettered power of these men to print currency at a rate that was unimagined just a few short years ago.

The idea that all paper assets could, and probably will, become worthless is an idea that almost no one can accept. The fact is that government issued fiat paper money has a limited life span; at some point, it always becomes worthless, or dies. It can take many years and when it unfolds the people who are in the middle of it are in complete and total shock. In order to understand this more clearly, it's important to think of this in terms of a wealth community.

This concept is not based simply upon a nation's currency, but in terms of their overall economic, social, religious, education, health and political success.

When money dies other modes of trade and earning inevitably arise. Assets like energy, including oil, hydropower, methanol, and wind emerge from behind investments and securities and become singularly important to the day-to-day survival of a country. Precious metals, things that are limited in supply, fuel a greater demand and become a temporary currency of their own. Food and the ability to acquire it promptly are foremost considerations. Medicines can determine whether an epidemic thrives or dies – likewise it determines who will survive. Even simple things, like sewing thread can become a valued commodity.

A gold rush occurs when people hear that precious metal has been found. They then rush to seek their fortune. Gold in of itself can be used as money. Mining, in its simplest form, becomes a viable profession. If you doubt this, take a few minutes to watch the television show "Bering Sea Gold" to consider the reality of literally scooping your financial support off the ocean floor. Take that one step further, however, and consider the other industries that spring up in support. Merchants who offer supplies for the miner prosper. Gold assaying becomes a valued profession. Transporting the heavy metal must be done by water from this remote location. The concept of gold being discovered brings in hopeful miners who need transportation, food, shelter, clothing, knowledge and medical care.

When a money dies there is a direct dissolution of years of education and internship among the standard professions. Who has need of a manager where there is nothing to manage. And what of the art, history or English major? The university whose enrollment is non-existent has no need of highly educated professors. If we cannot buy automobiles we do not need their designers or engineers. Plastic surgeons must put aside their laser gimmicks and tend to sewing up wounds. You do not need a chef when no one is in the restaurant.

The result is that an economic shift occurs between long accepted industries and those new ones, derived from the simple concept of…need. People no longer think about purchasing items that they want, they are driven strictly by the concept of need.

A recession/depression is possibly the best time to launch a new business or to expand an existing one. It's also a great time to get ahead in your career. This may sound counterintuitive but during those times, people get scared and start cutting back on expenses. They modify their needs and it becomes rather chic to "do without." Certain businesses flourish. Take, for example, the health and beauty aids manufacturer. Cosmetics are well known to command exorbitant markups and profit margins. The $10.00 bottle of red nail polish contains one ounce in a weighted bottle while for the same money we can purchase an entire gallon of tinted gloss paint. The concept is the same. In a dead economy not only does the consumer have no desire to paint their nails, but these funds must be allocated to basic necessities such as shampoo and soap. In such economies the store brands flourish and the value of companies who make them skyrocket as demand grows.

We also become more sensitive to receiving genuine value. When we spend money, we want to make sure we're getting a fair deal. Businesses that provide genuine value can actually do better during a recession. More people will flock to those businesses in tough times, while the fluff businesses will become more and more paranoid.

Some people choose unwise methods to make money, often involving bad decisions in an attempt to earn more money. They buy into fool-hardy moneymaking programs, join and promote useless MLM schemes, and fall prey to scammers. But they keep getting drawn into trying to make money without providing any real value, which is unsustainable. Instead of focusing on trying to make more money, we all need to put more time and energy into creating and delivering real value. We need to find ways to give people what they really want and/or need.

We are a nation of consumers. This means we are currently focused on acquiring goods and the consumption of resources. This is not a value proposition. The U.S. became a great nation because it was a country of producers. There's a sign on a bridge leading into Trenton, New Jersey, which was once a manufacturing stalwart. It reads, "Trenton makes, the world takes." This is a testament to what it takes to become a great nation. Contrast this with the Trenton of today. Most employees in Trenton work for the state government. Unemployment is over 13 percent. A large portion of the city's population collects welfare, disability payments and is otherwise dependent upon the government for sustenance. A country that creates nothing but bureaucrats, welfare recipients and other non-producers cannot stay great or become great once again.

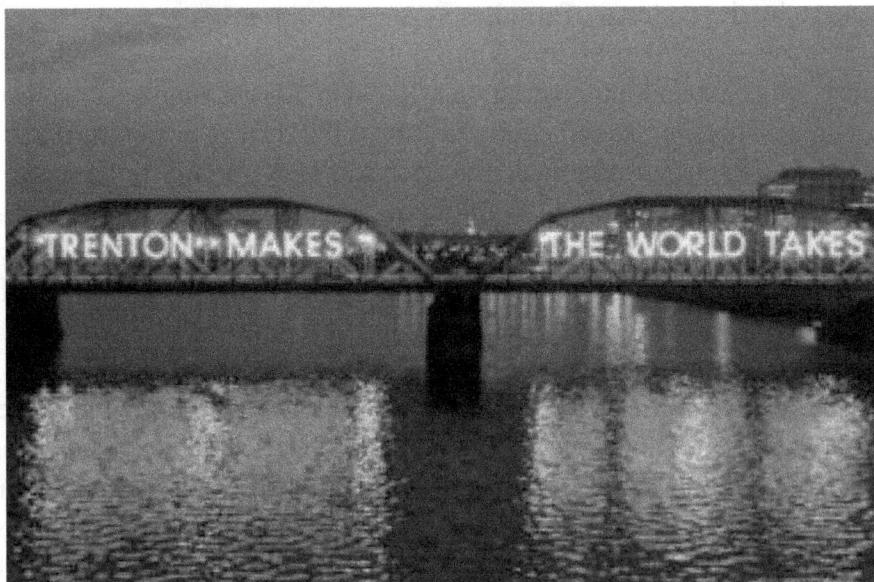

This is where our personal values and the nation's values are so important. Right now our primary concerns are based on acquiring material possessions – to the point that we not only accumulate more than we need, but at some point we begin to replace what we already have with a "newer" version. The result is a flourishing economy in second-hand retail. Consider eBay and the Goodwill explosions of growth, as well as public storage centers and TV shows that exploit the sale of abandoned storage lockers.

Money is assumed to be the way to spend life happily and free of tensions. Poverty commands little respect. However, acquiring wealth the right way, by providing value and producing must again become the American Way. If we are successful in returning to our humble origins, our country will regain its greatness and the world will be a better place. If we don't, freedom will continue to be diminished and we suffer the loss of the American dream for generations to come.

Finding Safety in an Unsafe World

We are all looking for safety and security. It is not just a want, but a need, a constant and necessary solution to our instinctive and evolutionary demands. However, security has different definitions. Some of us feel safe when we are in a permanent relationship, have children, have paid off a house, have graduated from college, reached a monetary goal or simply lost 50 pounds.

We crave the security of knowing what the day will hold. We rely on others to be our guides. How often do we wake up and flip on the television to see what the weather will be? Do we simply walk to the door and open it – to feel the temperature and gauge the cloud cover ourselves? No, we feel a sense of importance in knowing that it will be 20 degrees warmer at noon and it's likely to rain that evening. This information does little to make us change our plans, or even our intended wardrobe, and yet we feel ill equipped if we haven't checked the forecast before we leave home.

Fifty years ago people settled in their easy chairs in the early evening and tuned in news commentators like Walter Cronkite. His authoritative, conservative manner made us feel at ease in an era spooked by the Cold War and the looming prospect of nuclear extinction. He did not render personal opinion, and kept a journalistic distance from anything that could be considered hearsay. Today, our most-often consulted source of news is Twitter, which relies completely on unsubstantiated hearsay and rumor. Our reference source is the Internet; a collection of uninformed non-professionals who often profit in either coin or ego by circulating opinion that holds little relevance or reliability.

Yet we have not relinquished our need for predictability and pattern. This is where we get our semblance of security. The concept of a blue chip stock has changed dramatically.

Does this shift frighten you? Do you feel as though you are in a free fall and lack the reliable sources needed to guide your future actions and investments? You are not alone.

Twitter, horoscopes and meteorology are not the foundations upon which you can protect your family's survival. We live in an era of terrorism; much of it is psychological rather than physical. Governments and the elites are constantly trying to keep us in a state of fear so we'll be more accepting of the latest restriction on our freedoms. Consider the drug industry. Spend an hour watching the evening news – a time slot that caters to mature adults. You will see a cavalcade of pharmaceutical commercials that invite you to discuss your health with your doctor on a peer-to-peer basis. Use the information offered in the commercial to suggest to this licensed professional that perhaps your arthritis could be better helped if you tried a specific drug. We will not take into consideration that the drug is just out of testing and therefore at the beginning of its patent protection – making its product testing costs the responsibility of your health insurance company, or your own pocketbook. The medication is not guaranteed to cure or relieve anything – it's only a suggestion. While you're considering it, you should remember that it can have side effects and these can range from mild irritation to, in some cases, death. Life itself has become a risk.

So where do we gain security in life? What is the center lane, the norm, the sure thing? There is none – save the oft-quoted death and taxes. In an insecure economic climate, even taxes have a questionable future.

There are some certainties in life. Gold represents one of these in that it is an ever-present resource. Regardless of whether it is coined, made into jewelry or used in electronics, it is recoverable. Once oil and gas are burned they cannot be recovered. Corn and wheat are consumed and their byproducts are not edible. Land can be sold beyond reach and has no value unless it is desirable. If you do not believe this, talk to the millions who have been rendered homeless by the banking collapse that affected the housing market. Educations are only worth what a person is worth in an ever-changing economy, which could be little or nothing, in spite of their high priced degree. If that leaves you doubting, talk to the highly paid journalists who are wandering around while paper and the printed word disappear.

Gold has been eternally respected, throughout ancient civilization up to the present. It is rare and therefore valuable. Whether the gold has been designed into jewelry or left in bullion form, it has an innate value that is not lessened or affected by its transformation.

It is, quite succinctly, the standard.

The other certainty is you. You have the capacity to learn and understand the tenets of what has been said here. You can depend on your own awareness to guide your decisions – assuming they are educated decisions.

You are resilient and can open your mind to these basic premises and will consequently be well prepared for survival.

Planning—It's All
We Can Do

This is the year Americans elect a president. Certain rules apply and when the incumbent is seeking re-election, you can be certain that there will be filters in place when it comes to the state of the economy in particular. No one wants to admit they have failed.

Among the issues occupying the Republican debates, was the economy. While each of the candidates had an individual plan for recovery, the consensus was that we are in trouble and it's going to take more than just one individual's plan to kick start us on the road to fiscal health.

Finance is a science of numbers. The premise that numbers do not lie may hold true, but certainly not for the people whose job it is to report those numbers. They do lie, often and believably. It is not just for self-preservation that they do so; it is for the preservation of a way of life that we have come to expect as our due. We work hard, save, plan and for what? So that we know we will be taken care of after retirement.

Yet the food banks are busily handing out supplies to those seniors whose retirement security was undermined by the Madoffs of the world. Our president is intent upon handing out the nation's security in one stimulus package after another. Our election will be based not on who is the better candidate, but who is most believable.

This is because we rely so strongly on faith. We must survive simply because we must survive. If we, as a country, do not survive, who will help the rest of the world? Who will be on hand when a dictator has gotten out of control? Who will feed the hungry when a drought robs its fields? Who will bail out a foreign power because to sacrifice it means to sacrifice a platform from which to fight for freedom? Freedom from whom?

The commodities that make up our hierarchy of critical need are based on trends. We cannot rely on the price of oil or the real estate on the coast of California. Upon what, then, do we rely?

Some forecasters will tell you to go out and buy a gun. You will need it to protect your family from roving bands of hungry neighbors who saw

121

you carry in those cases of beans you bought at the grocery. Those who used to be considered rogues will sell you dried food and give you a quick tutorial on building your own sun panels for collecting energy. You can find any number of windmill kits and companies willing to build underground shelters with their own water and ventilation systems. This sort of a structure isn't intended for defense against nuclear attack, by the way ... but defense from your neighbor's hungry children.

It is a gray and cloudy horizon we see in the distance. Some investors are warning that the current weak recovery is but a last gasp and economic collapse is certain. Not going to happen? Check out Zimbabwe or WWII Germany and talk to people whose lives did just that. Do you suppose they planned on it?

You can. You can do just that – you can plan on the very real forecast that it is going to rain. The storm will collapse everything that has value as you know it. The basics of life will be your guiding light each and every morning you awaken. What will you eat? Is there food? Is there fuel for heat? Is there medicine?

How can you plan for this? It's much more than burying a hundred cases of bottled water. That may be fine if you plan to spend this one and only life in a hole in the ground. If, however, you want to move to a warmer climate where there is no need for heating oil, or you want to get a doctor to take care of your sick child ... you're going to need to be portable and soluble. You need to invest in the one thing that has never changed its perception since it first came into a man's hand.

"When money stops flowing to the man on the street, blood starts flowing in the street," says trend forecaster, Gerald Celente.

You must ask yourself just what it will take to convince you? If history does not do it, will you wait until the day you hold that sick child in your arms to realize you should have listened?

Isn't it time you based your life on the standard of gold?

There have been times when gold has not been the most valuable metal. Other elements in the platinum group have risen above it in terms of their price, but never in their cultural value. The history of gold has made it the most precious metal in the world, even if it is not always the most expensive. The gold standard has been the basis of many currencies.

War always has a tremendous economic impact on a national finances. Many nations, after losing a war, have gone broke and were required to financially restructure. This was the case of Germany after World Wars I and II. During the conflict the population is often called upon to make great sacrifices in the name of victory and solvency. Central banks have historically provided financing for war efforts. Central banks have the ability to provide funding for both sides to the war, reaping huge profits. In the event of an outright defeat by one party and victory by the other, the bank might suffer some losses due to the loser's inability to pay. But the inevitable prolonging of such a war would ensure higher profits would be as high as possible.

Conclusion

The problem with finishing a work such as this, is that history never stops being written. It is now July of 2012 and the global credit bust/depression has been going strong since late 2007 early 2008. What started out in the U.S. as a "manageable" problem in the sub-prime housing sector, soon spread around the world and has brought down numerous once august financial institutions such as Lehman Brothers, Bear Stearns, Merrill Lynch and many others. Many of storied financial houses today exist in name only, having been forcibly merged into "healthier" banks, in an effort to prevent a complete implosion of the global financial system.

In the end, every business deemed "Too Big to Fail" got bailed out, with over $16 trillion dollars being printed by the Federal Reserve, out of thin air, and shipped off to banks and corporations around the world. And no systemic changes or management changes were required by the Fed or the Treasury. It was status quo anti-collapse. And all the while, the management kept getting their oversized and undeserved bonuses.

While the banks and their wealthy management got bailed out, neither average American nor small business got any help at all. These efforts have been unfair to working Americans, but more importantly, they have greatly damaged the free market and the "real" economy. In earlier times, no one was Too Big to Fail and these large financial institutions would have been liquidated and erased from memory. Now, no politician is willing to cross his Wall Street Masters and propose such a solution.

We're in a debt crisis, where obligations undertaken in better times cannot possibly be paid off. So what happens to the debt? There are only three choices, inflation, default or forgiveness. Inflation is the most damaging to the social fabric and when taken to its logical hyper inflationary conclusion, the middle class is destroyed. A default, either managed or cascading, can have salutary effects, as in the case of Iceland. They refused to payoff the banksters, defaulted on all their bonds and closed banks and replaced managements. The result; their economy has started to grow once again. And finally, forgiveness, or the debt jubilee. The government would pass a proclamation forgiving certain debts in whole or in part. This would require the recapitalization or replacement of the large banks, which would have to be done at the same time. Remember that one person's debt is someone else's asset, more than likely a Too Big to Fail bank's. A reversion back to sound money would make this option viable and the preferred course.

As we've seen, central banks exist to help the banks survive. They were created simply to act as the lender of last resort to insure that the banking system would stay afloat in times when the loans went bad and banks were under-capitalized and over-leveraged. And in 2008 they performed this function admirably. Unfortunately, their management is derived from the ranks of Too Big to Fail banks, especially Goldman Sachs. And the politicians who are supposed to put the brakes on this banking cartel have had their finances and their fortunes underwritten by this same corrupt financial sector. So the possibility of wringing excesses out of the system while allowing the act of creative destruction, which keeps capital flowing to its best use, is not happening. And since an unlimited number of currency units can be created at will, due to the lack of any backing for the dollar or limitation on the supply of them, the system must eventually fail.

Which leaves you with only one choice. *Wipe The Street Clean—A Guide To Real Wealth*

www.ingramcontent.com/pod-product-compliance
Lightning Source LLC
Chambersburg PA
CBHW062023200326
41519CB00017B/4909